THE UNCOMMON COLLEGE ESSAY

THE UNCOMMON COLLEGE ESSAY

An Approachable Guide to an Intimidating Process

Stacey Brook

BLOOMSBURY ACADEMIC
NEW YORK • LONDON • OXFORD • NEW DELHI • SYDNEY

BLOOMSBURY ACADEMIC

Bloomsbury Publishing Inc, 1359 Broadway, New York, NY 10018, USA
Bloomsbury Publishing Plc, 50 Bedford Square, London, WC1B 3DP, UK
Bloomsbury Publishing Ireland, 29 Earlsfort Terrace, Dublin 2, D02 AY28, Ireland

BLOOMSBURY, BLOOMSBURY ACADEMIC and the Diana logo are trademarks of Bloomsbury Publishing Plc

First published in the United States of America 2025

Copyright © Stacey Brook, 2025

Cover image © iStock/Varijanta
Cover design by Enterline Design Services

All rights reserved. No part of this publication may be: i) reproduced or transmitted in any form, electronic or mechanical, including photocopying, recording or by means of any information storage or retrieval system without prior permission in writing from the publishers; or ii) used or reproduced in any way for the training, development or operation of artificial intelligence (AI) technologies, including generative AI technologies. The rights holders expressly reserve this publication from the text and data mining exception as per Article 4(3) of the Digital Single Market Directive (EU) 2019/790.

Bloomsbury Publishing Inc does not have any control over, or responsibility for, any third-party websites referred to or in this book. All internet addresses given in this book were correct at the time of going to press. The author and publisher regret any inconvenience caused if addresses have changed or sites have ceased to exist, but can accept no responsibility for any such changes.

Library of Congress Cataloging-in-Publication Data is available

ISBN: PB: 979-8-7651-5105-1
       ePDF: 979-8-7651-5106-8
       eBook: 979-8-7651-5107-5

Typeset by Integra Software Services Pvt. Ltd.
Printed and bound in the United States of America

For product safety related questions contact productsafety@bloomsbury.com.

To find out more about our authors and books visit www.bloomsbury.com and sign up for our newsletters.

CONTENTS

Introduction 1

1. Does the College Essay Even Matter? Getting a Lay of the Land 3

2. What Is a Personal Essay? Decoding the Purpose of the College Application's Personal Statement 11

3. How Do You Find the Magic Topic? Embracing the Backwards Brainstorm 23

4. How Do You Conquer the Blank Page? Freewriting Your Face Off 39

5. How Do You Capture—and Keep!—a Reader's Attention? Sculpting Your Story 55

6. What About the Finishing Touches? Polishing to Perfection 71

7. What Are Those OTHER Admissions Essays? A Quickie Guide to Supplemental Essays, the UC Personal Insight Questions, and More 83

8. What If You're Doing It Wrong? Myths, Misconceptions, and Mistakes 105

9. Am I Going to Lose My Mind? Staying Sane During a Stressful Process 115

10 Do You Think These People Are Boring? Essay Examples and How to Use—or Not Use—Them 125

Stacey's Final Thoughts 139
Acknowledgments 140
Index 142
About the Author 148

INTRODUCTION

Who Am I and How Do I Know That You Are Not Boring? Meet the Expert

Think you're the most boring person in the room? Think again. The most boring person in the room is, by definition, not boring. That person is, in fact, the best at being boring, which is inherently interesting.

So if you're a student preparing to write your college essay and you think you're the most boring person on the planet, I hate to disappoint you, but you're not. *(No one is.)*

That's not to say it's easy to pinpoint what makes you compelling, especially to an outsider like an admissions officer. Identifying your most distinctive qualities is all about perspective. Sure, some students will come to the college essay-writing process with an obvious story to tell. But more often, students are working with a familiar set of teenage experiences that require close examination and creative unpacking to reveal unique viewpoints and traits worth highlighting. Sometimes displaying your strengths involves reframing seemingly ordinary events from unexpected angles. Often the smallest details and anecdotes can provide insight into your mindset and motivation, revealing who you are and how you think about the world. Identifying methods for communicating your distinct perspective is often the difference between a generic college essay and one that is, at its core, *uncommon. (Like you!)*

After working with over a thousand students in my more than twenty years as a personal college essay consultant and the founder and chief advisor at College Essay Advisors (CEA), I have never met a student who doesn't have a story—or, more often, multiple stories—worth telling. I consider it a truth at this point that each candidate is undeniably, verifiably interesting. But my simply asserting this truth doesn't make it easy for a student to believe it or give them the tools they need to tap into their inner magic.

Most likely if you're picking up a book about how to write the college essay, it's because you don't know where or how to start the writing process. Should you read a thousand essays of former applicants, taking notes on the merits of each one; or make a list of all of your greatest accomplishments as dictated by your ninety-five-year-old grandmother? *(She has a lot of positive things to say!)* Should you sit and stare at your computer for forty-five minutes in a state of sheer panic, wondering how you'll ever get through the daunting task of trying to distill your entire life and its meaning into 650 poignant words that will immediately make an admissions officer want to adopt you as their own? *Should you just give up?*

Probably *(definitely)* not.

But that's why I'm here. Through my signature, four-step Uncommon College Essay Approach (which includes Backwards Brainstorming, Freewriting Your Face Off, Sculpting Your Story, and Polishing to Perfection), savvy advice, positive reinforcement, and real student examples, I can help you transform your blank screen into a thoughtfully crafted admissions essay you can confidently send to the school of your dreams. So let's leave the fear and self-doubt and pressure to succeed behind and dive into the world of personal exploration and creative storytelling—together.

With love and *(many)* conversational parentheticals,
Stacey Brook

1 Does the College Essay Even Matter? Getting a Lay of the Land

Aside from the concern that an applicant may not have anything worth writing about in their admissions essay, one of the most common questions I hear from students and parents alike is: "Does the college essay really matter?"

In a word: Yes. *(In another: Obviously!)*

The college essay is an integral tool in distinguishing yourself from other, similarly qualified applicants. It is one of the few opportunities you will have to speak to admissions in your own voice; to showcase your passions and motivations; and to exhibit a hint of the personality that might come across if an admissions officer were sitting in a room with you.

Over the past decade and change, the admissions industry has transformed its approach to assessing student applications, favoring a holistic review that rewards quality over quantity in a student's academic and extracurricular endeavors. Accordingly, there's been a decided shift away from standardized testing as an iron-clad mechanism for measuring achievement and, as of 2024, over two thousand schools enacted a "test-optional" policy that allows students to apply without submitting standardized test scores. That is not to say you shouldn't try your hand at filling in those little bubbles *(that's how it still works, right?)*—especially if you perform well in a high-pressure testing environment—but admissions is *(in my opinion, rightfully)* recognizing that they will miss out on stellar candidates if they adhere only to old formulas, and that self-expression can offer a revealing insight into a student's true value.

That said, the college essay isn't a magic bullet; if you don't have the qualifying grades (and test scores) for the institutions to which you are applying, the essay cannot necessarily make up for all that lost ground—but it can balance any seeming holes in your transcript and résumé. It gives students the opportunity to reveal their unique strengths to admissions, and it can certainly be the factor that breaks a tie and pushes a student in contention into the "yes" pile.

Perhaps most importantly, the college essay is one of the few humanizing efforts in a process that has become increasingly robotic. Show admissions you're a living, breathing person with thoughts and feelings, interests and ambition—unless, of course, your ambition is to turn yourself into some kind of AI prototype for the advancement of science and human progress, and then by all means, embrace the robot within. *(And please write about it!)*

I'm sure you're still asking yourselves the following:

- Where does the essay fit into the scheme of the college application as a whole? *(Somewhere important!)*
- Do admissions officers even read these things? *(Yes!)* And even if they do…
- What can you accomplish in 650 words? *(A lot!)*

SO WHY DOES THE COLLEGE ESSAY MATTER?

Before we get to your burning questions, let's take a look at the admissions landscape over the past few years. Unless you've recently awoken from a cryogenic freeze, you're probably aware that college admissions has become increasingly competitive; more students are applying to college than ever, millions hailing from all over the world. *(That's a lot!)* Because of this steady uptick, which is also a result of students applying to more schools because of test-optional policies, the acceptance rates at the country's most elite academic institutions have decreased dramatically. For the past decade, Harvard and Stanford have been hovering at acceptance rates of (or under) 4 percent to 5 percent. *(That's not a lot!)* With acceptance levels dipping into the low single-digit percentages for top-tier colleges, it is clear that the competition for some of the country's elite schools is at an all-time high. This, in turn, has made it more challenging for students applying to any of the top 50, 100, 200, even 500 ranked colleges in the United States. Regardless of a school's ranking, where you go doesn't matter nearly as much as what you do when you get there, and mastering the college essay will not only help you get into your target school, but it will also prepare you to succeed once you're there.

The point is this: securing admission to your dream school is more challenging than it has ever been, no matter where you want to go.

The students who do get into the colleges of their choice use all the tools at their disposal. And long after three years of grades are filed, activities are invested in, and the SATs/ACTs are taken, the college essay remains the only major element of the application you can impact during the application process itself. But if you want to cook up the best college essay in town, you have to come to the kitchen armed with your best ingredients, a killer recipe, and a resilient spirit ready for the occasional improvisational exercise. The college essay has the potential to represent not just who you are and where you've been in your journey to college, but also who you might become both on campus and beyond. For this reason, the college essay can be an epic weapon in your arsenal, as convincing as a magic mirror, as sharp as a samurai sword, and as endearing as an entire basket of puppies. Admissions officers love puppies. *(*Please note, this has not yet been proven under perfect laboratory conditions.)*

So, here's the amazing news: Mastery of this assignment gives you a distinct advantage in the admissions game. And while it may seem daunting at first, the college essay is absolutely conquerable.

WHERE DOES THE ESSAY FIT INTO THE OVERALL APPLICATION?

While the essay is a potent piece of the puzzle, it is important to remember that it is but one of the crucial components of your college application.

There is also the transcript, which is undeniably one of the top factors in an admissions officer's assessment of any applicant. Even this straightforward index of your achievements is evaluated based on a complex combination of characteristics, including your grades in advanced classes, the strength of your curriculum, and of course, your grade point average (GPA).

Then, who doesn't love to look at some standardized test scores, the measurement of how well a student can memorize vocabulary and apply a contained set of concepts and equations after eating a good breakfast and trying not to puke from anxiety?

Next come teacher and guidance counselor recommendations, which provide admissions with outsider views on a student's drive and personality.

The lovely people deciding your academic fate also review a detailed list of your extracurricular activities. *(Hopefully those four years of birdwatching paid off!)*

Before admissions officers look at your college essay, they know the names and ages of all your siblings *(if you have them)*, your class rank, and your family income. By the time they get to your essay, they probably even know your dog's name and your shoe size *(and maybe even your dog's shoe size)*. These are all things that, no matter how good a student you are, tend to overlap with the life circumstances and accomplishments of your closest competitors.

What admissions *doesn't* know before they read your college essay is what it would be like to spend time with or talk to you in person. Would you immediately launch into an impassioned dissertation about your latest micro-obsession? Would you point out recently published discoveries about the constellations? Would you notice the opal on your admissions officer's finger because you're obsessed with gemstones and make jewelry in your spare time? What motivates you? What are your passions? Your future goals? Your weird obsessions? Would you bring a positive attitude to campus? How are you going to contribute to the community? This is your chance to show admissions how you think about the world and what's really important to you. *(Looks like I'm writing my college admissions essay about pasta!)*

The college essay also provides your one and only opportunity to speak to admissions in your own voice. You need to use this window to showcase your personality and highlight how you are different from the competition in a way that is highly personal. *(Doesn't that sound SO EASY?! Don't worry—I'm going to help.)*

"Okay, fine," you're saying. "I get it. *In theory*, the essay is important in the context of the application, but…"

DO ADMISSIONS OFFICERS EVEN READ THESE THINGS?

Let's indulge in a brief thought experiment. Imagine you're a college admissions officer. You're pumped to dig into your pile of new applicants. You're jazzed to see what the students of the new admissions cycle might bring to your academic community. You're…oh, my God, you're responsible for reviewing over a thousand applications per season. You realize this shakes out to about fifty applications per day. You need to flip through 6.25 of these babies in an hour. This gives you about nine minutes to review a student's entire application, and about two to three minutes to devote to the college essay. You regularly spend more time scrolling through social media during commercials than you do reading a student's college admissions essay. You spend more time each day daydreaming about what it would be like to walk with dinosaurs *(you really like dinosaurs)* than you do on one student's personal statement. It's a good thing each student has spent six months pulling 650 words out of the depths of their souls, polishing each phrase to a high shine so you could spend more time opening a stubborn bag of potato chips than you do on each of their college essays.

No one said life was fair.

What does this mean for you, dear applicant?

It means that you have less time than you ever imagined to capture an admissions officer's attention. It means that if you're going to make an impression with your carefully crafted words, you better make it fast, and you better make that mark deep. It means that your college admissions essay better be at least as entertaining as a cute puppy video and tastier than a bag of Stacy's Pita Chips. *(Admittedly that last one is not that hard.)* It means you better put in the effort to make sure your admissions essay breaks through the noise and hits admissions officers where it counts. But where *does* it count? How can you make an admissions officer feel all the right *feels* about you as a candidate?

WHAT CAN YOU REALLY ACCOMPLISH IN 650 WORDS?

There are a few things you should be specifically aiming for, and all of them are easy enough to accomplish.

Make Yourself Memorable

In advertising, the idea of making yourself memorable is called "branding." Celebrities often call it "star power." What it really boils down to is finding something about yourself, your experiences, and what you have to offer to the world that is instantly recognizable and easily recollected. What will make you stand out in a sea of similarly qualified applicants?

If a group of admissions officers is sitting around the decision table, surveying students with similar GPAs and activity lists, what will make the one reading your essay grab your application, stand up, and say, "Take her! Take the trapeze artist with the fear of heights!" or "Don't forget the coder who made the carrot dance!" An admissions officer should be able to easily recall details that are emblematic of your personality and that are representative of who you are at your core.

Tell Admissions Something They Don't Know

You should use these essays as an opportunity to say something that hasn't been said. What do you feel? What is important to you? What do you value? Maybe you talk about the bonding that occurs in morning car rides with your mom, or your nerdy love of building elaborate model zoos in your bedroom. It could be interesting to discuss how you effortlessly navigate what could be an all-consuming allergy to processed foods *(I am so sorry about that, by the way)*, or maybe compare your talents and inner qualities to your favorite flowers. The students who are most successful reveal something to admissions officers that they would not otherwise be able to find on your transcript.

Now, this doesn't mean you can't write about something that already appears on your activity list or in your academic report; what it means is that your essay shouldn't be about the mission of Habitat for Humanity, or what you accomplished in your community service hours for that organization. Admissions doesn't want you to recount awards earned or tasks completed; rather, they are interested in how your time with Habitat for Humanity impacted your life on a personal level. What unexpected experience did you have there that made you a more complete and interesting person? Tell them about working alongside a deaf volunteer and how learning about how she engages with the world inspired you to become a sign language interpreter at your school. If you can't tell a story that is personal and revelatory, you should consider looking elsewhere for a topic. *(Try your bedroom dresser, second drawer from the bottom.)*

Put Your Personality on Display

Are you studious and curious? Are you sensitive and brave? Are you determined? Are you funny? *(Are you hungry? Have a donut.)* These qualities should shine through in your final essay. No matter the topic, an admissions officer should feel as if they've been offered a giant slice of your essence. Family members and friends should be able to recognize your voice.

Prove Your Value as a Community Member

As a member of a higher academic institution, your talents, skills, and qualities don't exist in a bubble. Admissions wants to know not only that you care about furthering your own education and realizing your own potential, but also that you will contribute to the larger community. This is why themes like generosity, sincerity, and self-reflection are so important. Schools want to know you will have a positive influence on those around you and that your gifts will be shared with the other great minds they choose for your cohort.

Showcase Your Basic Writing and Storytelling Abilities

Not all students are drawn to expressing themselves on the page, and schools will probably expect more nuanced writing and storytelling from their aspiring English majors than they will from, say, their aspiring engineers. *(Though I know a lot of engineers who can also tell a great story.)* But in a world where people communicate primarily using the written word, even if it's predominantly through email and text, it is crucial for students to have mastered the basics of writing and storytelling. And *(spoiler alert!)* you will have to write in college. Still, I know you have the determination and persistence to rise to the challenge. Find a story that is memorable and one that naturally exudes authentic personality, and good storytelling will follow. Attention to detail and solid proofreading, which we will cover later in this book, will take care of the rest.

2 What Is a Personal Essay? Decoding the Purpose of the College Application's Personal Statement

You may be wondering, of all the tasks admissions could ask you to complete, why are they asking you to compose this writing-centric, hyper-personal representation of yourself? You might even be thinking, what exactly *is* a personal statement/personal essay?

This is where, as a lover of the written word whose very favorite vehicle of expression is first-person storytelling, I geek out. I believe the personal essay is one of the most effective modern vehicles of independent expression. *(Nerd!)* If executed well, it contains all the elements for sincere, compelling storytelling, enabling the writer to highlight their unique perspectives and experiences while presenting them in a way that deeply resonates with the reader, illuminates a fresh, valuable point of view, or both.

For those of you who aren't word nerds, or who are looking for a less biased, more practical explanation, let's talk about the core elements of a personal essay and why this form is so valuable as an assessment tool for admissions officers.

WHAT IS A PERSONAL ESSAY?

Most college applications ask students to submit a "personal essay" or "personal statement," terms that I will be using here interchangeably. The personal essay is different from most of the assignments you've conquered in your academic career thus far: It isn't that research paper that required you to impeccably cite four hundred sources related to mitosis, and it isn't a reflection paper on how *Our Town* is a metaphor for *your* town. *(I wrote that one and aced it, by the way. Still proud.)* Personal essay-writing is a form of expression that turns the focus back on the writer. It uses a first-person perspective in which the writer addresses themselves as "I." Most academic essays—the ones you have written for your history and English classes—default to the third-person perspective, in which the writer communicates as an outside observer, removing themselves from the action. Consider these two sentences:

First person: As I explained the essence of personal essays to future readers, my fingers flew across the keys.
Third person: As she explained the essence of personal essays to future readers, Stacey's fingers flew across the keys.

It's a rare occasion in which you are encouraged to use the word "I" with relative abandon, but that's exactly what admissions is asking you to do. Personal essays should be conversational in tone. They should read as you would sound if you were telling a story to a friend—assuming that story didn't involve a host of abbreviations *(srsly!)*, references to emojis *(I know, super sadface)*, and use of other weird internet language *(let that cook for a minute)*.

In addition to this stylistic adjustment, the personal essay also demands that you embark on a journey of self-reflection *(something teenagers love, universally)*. What have you done in your life, and what have these actions and adventures meant to you? What might they mean for your future? What do you like and why? In essence, *who are you*? These are not always obvious or comfortable questions to explore, and a good personal essay will approach the answers with a balance of confidence, sincerity, humility, and even a little humor. Achieving that balance is one of the most difficult aspects of the task at hand and something I will discuss in detail throughout this book.

There is an interesting side effect of trying to dig around and come up with a subject for your college admissions essay. If you do it right, the essay-writing process can help you get in touch with who you really are as a person as you home in on some of your educational, professional, and other life goals. At first, your experiences may seem to fall into the same buckets as everyone else's: "Things I accomplished in my after-school activities." "Where I spent my summer vacation." "Why I love Beyoncé." *(At least that's one of my defining characteristics.)* You could be tempted to discard valuable ideas as "clichéd," even though a new perspective on a well-worn subject can make for an enlightening peek into your *(legitimately fascinating)* world. Guess what—you're motivated! You like a challenge! You're side-splittingly funny! You really, really like puppies! *(Oh right, that's me again.)*

For this reason, among many others, one of my main goals is to transform the college essay-writing process from an exercise in self-torture to a conduit for self-examination and personal discovery.

THE DREADED PROMPTS (AND WHY THEY DON'T REALLY MATTER)

Aside from "Can I borrow the car," "Does she really like me," and "Does Proactiv really work," have any questions inspired as much angst for teenagers as the personal statement essay prompts?

Regardless of the application platform (the Common Application, the Coalition Application, schools' independent websites, and more), the personal statement prompts long have struck fear in the hearts of applicants. What does it mean to "share [your] background story?" Does admissions really want you to talk about "a time you failed?" What are these prompts really trying to inspire in the applicants responding to them?

In chapter 1, you learned that the personal statement can have a mighty impact on how an admissions officer views your application because it reveals things that are not reflected in your transcript and test scores. You know it's the only certain opportunity you will have to speak to admissions in your own voice.

But I didn't tell you these things to stack on the pressure and imbue you with college-essay-related dread and horror. *(Seriously, I didn't.)* In fact, there is no reason to be afraid. Not only are the personal statement prompts not scary, but also when it comes to your topic selection (as in, the selection of what you want to write about, specifically), the prompts themselves *don't actually matter*. More on that later.

First, let's talk logistics. More often than not, a student will have options, allowing them to choose one from a set of prompts and respond in about 650 words. (A notable exception is the University of California application, which asks students to respond to four out of eight "Personal Inquiry Questions" in 350 words each. This task is covered in more detail in chapter 7.)

The personal statement prompts can change from year to year, but generally their purpose is the same: to help students identify their defining experiences, memories, stories, philosophies, and more—and they *can* be helpful in that way. I suggest using them not as a strict guideline for brainstorming and storytelling, but rather as a launch point for idea generation. In other words, don't get too hung up on the prompts at first, especially if they're not sparking inspiration. There are many methods of searching for a compelling personal story to tell, and I am going to take you through some great ones in chapter 3. For now, consider a few common prompts from application cycles past (that likely have recognizable counterparts in present submission options) and let's identify what kinds of ideas these questions are trying to conjure in your beautiful brain.

THE BACKGROUND PROMPT

One of my favorite personal statement prompts throughout the years *(and you know it's hard for me to choose, because: nerd)*, which has consistently appeared on the Common Application in various iterations goes something like this:

> *Some students have a background, identity, interest, or talent that is so meaningful they believe their application would be incomplete without it. If this sounds like you, then please share your story.*

This prompt offers all the flexibility an applicant could ask for, with just enough direction to get those creative juices flowing. What about your history, personality, hobbies, or accomplishments might be worth highlighting for an admissions officer? It can be something as small as seeing an episode of a television show *(are you living life in the Upside Down?)* or as large as the struggle of moving to a foreign country *(especially if you had to leave behind grandma's cooking)*. The most important part is that your topic and/or perspective is dynamic and specific to you and no one else.

Some Questions to Ask Yourself as You Consider This Prompt

- What about your history, family, or background sets you apart from your peers?
- How do you see yourself? How do the people who are closest to you see you?
- What achievements or experiences have been integral in molding your character and ambitions?
- What, in your sixteen years on this earth, has shaped you into the person you are today?

At first glance, the "background prompt" can feel overwhelmingly general. But if you look closely and consider the question's elements one by one, you'll find helpful clues that can guide you in your personal-story detective work. For example, the fragment "background, identity, interest, or talent" is packed full of launch points *(four of them, to be exact)*.

Background

Your "background" can refer to a more traditional interpretation or something that has defined you over the course of your life. Do you come from a mixed family of Iranian, Lebanese, and Tennessean heritage? How did this impact your upbringing and the activities you chose to participate in? Do you know everything about the inner workings of trains because you grew up in a family of engineers who talked about regenerative braking at the dinner table? What are the challenges and rewards of having same-sex parents? Or of being raised by your siblings? Or of being part of a family made up of stepsisters and stepbrothers?

When I work with students, I often turn these prompts directly on myself to illustrate how I might approach them. For example, I am a born-and-bred Long Islander, now living in New York City, who has a love-hate relationship with my place of origin. *(Sorry to my fellow Strong Islanders.)* What is it like to be both proud of and a little self-conscious about where you come from? How might this complicated relationship with my place of origin have shaped me over time? If I interpret the word "background" a bit more creatively, I could write about being a *(mildly insufferable)* theater kid who saw her first Broadway musical (CATS!) at age ten, and whose father played *The Phantom of the Opera* soundtrack during family barbeques *(totally normal)*. How might these influences and the resulting performative streak have helped me with everything from accessing my writerly creativity to conquering public speaking? *(Or did it simply make me the annoying person who sings "Part of Your World" from* The Little Mermaid *at karaoke?)*

Notice that many of the elements I'm pulling from my life reference specific experiences, memories, or details. You don't have to know exactly what territory an essay will cover and what the ultimate message will be when considering these prompts. Think about the stories that come up at the dinner table over and over and memories that easily float to the surface. Valuable essay fodder lies in these oft-repeated streams of thought.

Identity

Now let's look at "identity." How do you actively define yourself? Is your wild, ever-changing hair color reflective of your explosive creativity? Are you an everyday scientist who conducts your own ecosystem experiments with the native flora and fauna in your backyard? Or a self-taught chef aiming to transform the world of tasty vegan cuisine? What are some things pretty much everyone who knows you associates with you? What do you love to do more than anything else in the world? No idea is too small at this point in the game: Playing arcade games for stuffed toys might not seem important in isolation, but maybe you can say something about it that links it to your more intangible personality characteristics. *(I bet you could.)*

Interests

What about "interests?" What excites you? It could be a random subject: For example, you know everything there is to know about every airplane you ever board. Or maybe it's an activity that most people wouldn't think to define as an interest, like people-watching. Again, the broad nature of this prompt allows you to define your interests in any way you want.

Talents

Similarly, "talents" can be defined as things you excel at, like competitive ice skating or cake decorating or solving the daily *New York Times* word puzzles *(obviously me)*. I also love when students interpret "talents" a bit more loosely. You can be talented at keeping your cool under pressure or at holding doors open for others.

***

Overall, this prompt is what I call a "choose-your-own-adventure" prompt. It has historically served as a fabulous catch-all for subjects that don't fit within the confines of the other prompt options. And remember, these prompts are meant to be starting points, inspiring you to access what defines you. You can choose to see these directives as perspective openers instead of restrictive instructions.

THE SETBACK/FAILURE PROMPT

Another prompt category I love is one that students often misinterpret. Here is an example of what it might look like:

> *The lessons we take from obstacles we encounter can be fundamental to later success. Recount a time when you faced a challenge, setback, or failure. How did it affect you, and what did you learn from the experience?*

I have always believed that essays about overcoming obstacles are most effective when they focus more on solutions than problems. Accordingly, an essay in response to this prompt should convey an applicant's reaction, outlook, and reflections when facing one of life's many hurdles, as opposed to a detailed account of the hurdle itself. Aim to showcase qualities like tenacity, courage, and humility. The obstacles you choose to explore can be as serious as being tormented by bullies, as ingrained as the food insecurity that has plagued your family for years, or as seemingly pedestrian as a mistake that cost you a tip while working at a coffeeshop. While the possibilities are almost endless, be careful not to choose challenges that may seem trite, like failing to ace an exam and/or snag tickets to that BTS concert, or that illustrate a lapse in good judgment, like that time you crashed your car or ate ten cupcakes in one sitting. *(Guilty!)* As long as you isolate an incident of trial in your life and demonstrate how you learned from it, this can be a rewarding prompt to explore.

Some Key Questions to Consider

- How do you respond to hardship?
- What qualifies as a challenge or setback in your life experience?
- Are you the kind of person who can naturally turn every event, positive or negative, into a learning experience? What anecdotes might illustrate this quality?
- What have been some of the major setbacks or failures you've encountered in your life? Was there a silver lining?

Did a live-in grandparent's fragile health lead to a role-reversal in which you discovered your talent for caretaking? Did a series of setbacks on your road to becoming a junior pilot introduce you to aerospace engineering and a goal of pursuing a future career at NASA? Did your failure to follow directions result in a botched home science experiment *(root beer explosion!)* and a newfound appreciation for a balance of creativity and planned procedure?

As a writer I am often *(very often)* rejected when submitting pieces for publication. I have learned to celebrate each rejection as proof that I am pushing myself to meet challenging goals. When have you experienced failure and how has this shown that you are someone committed to dusting yourself off and making the most of even the toughest situations? That is what this prompt is trying to draw out.

Overall, try to keep these stories as positive as possible. Remember, these essays are not contemplative musings on your toughest times or dwellings on the hiccups that populate everyday life *(though these things can certainly be touched upon)*; they are about overcoming obstacles and refusing to submit to life's greatest challenges.

THE BELIEFS PROMPT

This prompt requires a student to speak passionately about their values and ideology, which are often thorny subjects that can be difficult to condense into compact stories. It can be one of the hardest prompts to steer in a productive direction without devolving into preachy territory. This is also a more hazardous prompt than most, as students need to carefully assess the risks of championing beliefs that might be polarizing for the admissions officers reading their essay. Still, it is an inspiring prompt for some and worth considering. Here's how it might appear on an application:

Reflect on a time when you questioned or challenged a belief or idea. What prompted your thinking? What was the outcome?

A response to this prompt can be incisive and deeply personal, as it was for a student who wrote about standing up to her parents' outdated stance on feminism. Applicants who can articulate their thoughts and feelings while showcasing flexibility and openness to considering others' ideas will stand out as valuable additions to any cohort. If this prompt stands out to you because you have a very specific story to tell or opinion to voice, run with it.

Consider These Questions as You Think about This Prompt

- When have you held an unpopular opinion?
- Are you the kind of person who will stand up for what you believe in? How?
- What are your fundamental morals and values? Why?
- How does your passion for the things you believe in manifest?

Are you openly queer at a strict religious school? How has this affected your self-image and relationships? Did you join a demonstration that was broken up by the police? How did you react? Did you challenge the idea of romance as a women-exclusive genre by presenting an extensive research paper on the subject, launching a romance book club at school, and arranging the most elaborate, best-received Valentine's Day display your school has ever seen?

Personally, I challenge commonly held beliefs all the time—for example, the belief that there is such a thing as an off-limits essay topic! (More on this in chapter 8.)

Your essay does not have to discuss a fundamentally serious or groundbreaking issue (see the romance genre example above). What matters in your response to this prompt is that you have strong convictions about the idea you are trying to convey, and that you examine the personal effects of your belief(s) on your life and world. Thus, the beliefs essay can be a great vehicle for showcasing your compassion, influence, and passions to admissions.

THE ACCOMPLISHMENT PROMPT

At face value, this prompt might conjure up visions of trophies and blue ribbons, but there are a few things to note when unpacking it:

Discuss an accomplishment, event, or realization that sparked a period of personal growth and a new understanding of yourself or others.

Note that the words "accomplishment" and "event" are open to interpretation *(as with the four helpful launchpads from the background prompt)*. This means that a response to this question can tackle anything from a major event to a very small everyday occurrence. A formal event or accomplishment might include an obvious landmark like an anniversary or bar mitzvah to achievements like winning an award or earning a promotion. More informal examples could be as simple as first meeting a mentor, taking a car ride, or hearing a particularly meaningful song. I have often found that the smaller, less obvious events make for more surprising and memorable essays; but as with all the prompts, as long as you write with originality and put your unique twist on your topic, all ideas are fair game.

Reflecting on what you have learned and how you have grown will provide great insight for admissions, so your goal is to ensure that your essay reveals the intangible qualities that aren't apparent anywhere else on your application.

Some Other Things to Consider

- How do you respond to periods of adjustment? What prompts a change in your perspective?
- Have you had a "eureka" moment? When? How did it redirect your life thereafter?
- What moments in your life fundamentally molded you as a person?
- What experiences or lessons made you feel more adult or more capable?

Has your love of nature inspired you to start a charity to help save local endangered species? Did your desire to make a stronger shoelace launch you on an entrepreneurial adventure you never fully anticipated? Have you learned to love the football team playback sessions that force you to examine your missteps, invite constructive criticism, and orient yourself toward self-improvement? What did playing shuffleboard at a senior living center each week show you about the value of enjoyment over competition? How did this change the way you interact and connect with others?

Personally, I loved playing Ursula onstage in my sixth-grade *Disney Dazzle* showcase. It was the moment I realized that being a bold side character *(and a villain!)* could be more fun and interesting than playing the lead.

The most important things to look for when cataloging these moments are the elements of growth, maturity, and transformation. The event, accomplishment, or realization you describe should have helped you understand the world around you through a different, more nuanced lens.

THE PASSION PROMPT

One could argue *(and I will)* that college is primarily about the pursuit of knowledge, so you can imagine it would be quite beneficial for an admissions officer to read about your self-motivated learning, gaining a sense of how and why you are drawn to the things that interest you. This is why I love the "passion prompt" so much, which may appear like this on an application:

> *Describe a topic, idea, or concept you find so engaging that it makes you lose all track of time. Why does it captivate you? What or who do you turn to when you want to learn more?*

This prompt is trying to peek into your brain to learn how you process information and where you seek out inspiration. How tenacious are you when your curiosity is piqued? Your answer to this prompt should also illustrate the breadth or depth of your interests. For example, if you want to study sustainability, you might choose to discuss a concept that fuses your explorations into urban development, landscape architecture, and the environment. How consumed are you by the passion you are aiming to pursue in college?

Some Key Questions to Consider

- What floats your boat? Do you have an insatiable appetite for knowledge on a particular topic?
- How do you usually expand your knowledge when a new idea grabs you? Do you make a beeline to a favorite corner of the library or internet? Do you have a mentor who always answers your burning questions?
- What do you find satisfying about the process of learning, especially in your favorite subjects?

Did your discovery of open-source code inspire you to create a tech startup with your two best friends? What new ideas are you most excited to pursue with your new company? Did landing an internship at an investment bank prompt you to start your day by checking the markets? Did you found a mock trading club at your school to apply the expertise you've accumulated from culling through economic news and analysis? On any given Saturday, could we find you lost in a two-thousand-piece puzzle or beating your personal best Rubik's Cube solution time? Do you have an obsession with pizza so intense it led you to study the culinary arts and keep a pizza journal that documents the 700+ slices you've consumed thus far? *(I know someone who did this—really.)* How is pizza-making more scientific and/or artistic than the average person realizes?

As for me, I've been obsessed with Japan since I was a kid and have visited over thirty times, taken language lessons, learned the art of Japanese flower-arranging *(called ikebana)*, and become a self-proclaimed expert in playing crane/claw arcade games *(or UFO games, as they're called in Japan)*.

Whatever you're into, embrace it. Show your feathers. Let your freak flag fly *(within reason, obviously)*. This prompt is about the pursuit of knowledge of all kinds and your commitment to challenging yourself. Whether you're listening to classic LPs on your grandma's record player or calculating the perfect cheese blend for fondue, your enthusiasm about a subject should make admissions want to learn more about it—and you.

TOPIC OF YOUR CHOICE

I love this one because it's definitive proof of what I have been trying to communicate all along: that the prompts themselves don't really matter. *(At least not for the personal statement. They do for the supplemental essays, which I'll cover in chapter 7.)* Behold, a truly all-encompassing option you may encounter:

> *Share an essay on any topic of your choice. It can be one you've already written, one that responds to a different prompt, or one of your own design.*

While having the freedom to write about anything you want sounds great in theory, some students find—especially at the beginning of the brainstorming process—that this option is debilitating precisely because it offers *too much* choice. If that sounds familiar, use the other prompts to prompt *(see what I did there?)* your brainstorming. Ultimately, the personal statement prompts are broad enough to accommodate almost any story you want to tell, so go ahead and use them for some initial inspiration—but mostly focus on choosing the story you want to tell *first* and match that story to the prompts afterward. As I've found with pretty much every student I've guided over the past twenty-plus years, when you land on a truly valuable idea, the resulting essay will feel tailored to multiple prompts. *(And no, admissions doesn't care in the least which prompt you choose because again, the prompts don't really matter.)*

***

Now that we've explored some of the most common personal statement prompts and what they're really asking, I'm going to request you do something crazy: Pretend these prompts don't exist. Forget them forever. *(Okay, maybe not forever.)*

So if the prompts aren't that important, what *is* important? How do you decide what to write about?

First, grab yourself a cookie as a reward for getting this far. *(I'm going to get one, too!)* Then, we'll tackle the art of brainstorming in chapter 3.

3 How Do You Find the Magic Topic? Embracing the Backwards Brainstorm

I know this is going to be hard for you to believe, but no matter who you are, there is an amazing essay topic already inside of you. In fact, there are numerous compelling topics hiding in that adorable noggin of yours. Your challenge is to knock those gems loose so we can examine them and choose the ones that will shine under the scrutiny of the admissions microscope.

BUT, STACEY, WHAT IF I'M BORING?!!!!

Really though—everybody is boring! And none of us are boring! It's all about perspective and the ability to isolate and highlight the small details that will differentiate you in a competitive admissions landscape. In the end, everyone has a story to tell: Your really boring cousin has a story to tell *(Did you know she's obsessed with axolotls?)* and the guy who makes you your boba tea has a story to tell. *(What is it?)* Even Kim K. has a story to tell. Maybe she should stop telling her story. *(Is it possible to limit her to 650 words?)*

Speaking of which, what if, instead of feeling like you have nothing to say, you're like, *"OMG, STACEY, I HAVE SO MANY STORIES TO TELL!"* Well, you lucky duck, I will get to strategies for narrowing down your list to your best topics toward the end of this chapter. In fact, I'll walk you through *all* the stages of the brainstorming process, from getting started to "dos and don'ts" to sifting through your brilliant ideas.

But for now, know that, as we have discussed, the college essay aims to reveal something about you to admissions that they cannot glean from the rest of your application. Often these qualities are intangible measures of your character, passion, and motivation. They include but are not limited to the following:

Humor!
Creativity!
Curiosity!
Maturity. (Definitely a period after that one.)
Sincerity. (And that one.)
Introspection. (And that one.)
Motivation!
Originality!
Courage!
Ambition!
Resilience!
Positivity!

Are you funny? Do you ask a lot of questions? Do you push yourself? Are you sensitive? Are you selfless?

Of course, you don't need to showcase *all* these qualities in one essay. In fact, it is improbable that any one human being could show strength in all these areas. *(I should probably add "humble" to that list, eh?)* The point is, you are not trying to tell your life story in this college admissions essay, nor are you trying to encapsulate every single one of your admirable qualities in 650 words. An effective essay singles out two or three of these traits and uses a specific anecdote, metaphor, or other storytelling device to serve as a structure for housing and highlighting your talents. It emphasizes your human qualities, while also identifying you as someone worth remembering. The trick is to transform the brainstorming process from an exercise in academic pressure and existential crisis into a playtime for self-discovery and self-expression.

1. GETTING STARTED

In order to shift the focus of this process to exploration, we're going to come back to that strategy I mentioned in chapter 2 in which we actively decide to forget about the Common App Essay Prompts. *(The what? I've already forgotten them!)* This is how you'll kick off the Backwards Brainstorm, which is the first step in my handy-dandy Uncommon College Essay Approach. Here's how it works:

- Read through the Common App Essay prompts and get a sense of what kinds of questions admissions is asking. What type of qualities are they digging for? Where might they be hinting at a need for reflection?
- Put the prompts away. *(BYE!)* Brainstorm without considering them at all.

- Identify your best stories and ideas.
- Review the prompts again and consider this: Will the topics I'm considering satisfy any of the questions being asked?

Once you've dissected the Common App's prompts one by one and know what you're up against, and you also know that—at least for the time being—the specifics of those questions don't really matter, leave those prompts in the dust. What matters is the story YOU want to tell.

Once you have effectively thrown those to the side, like your Funko POP collection or any obligation you once felt to clean your room, it's time to start collecting your first ideas—good or bad, silly or serious, dinosaur-related or sadly not dinosaur-related. A good topic will capture something about how you see the world *("There are french fries everywhere!")*; emphasize your human qualities *("I am not a robot.")*; make you memorable in the mind of the admissions officer *(You want to be one step shy of haunting their dreams)*; or entertain *("Isn't this just like watching YouTube?")*.

In other words, your topic should reflect:

- how you think,
- how you interact with the people/world around you,
- why something is important to you, and
- why you do the things you do.

Your good idea is in there somewhere! You might just have to sift through a lot of sand to get to that nugget of gold.

So how should you get started? There are so many different ways to kickstart the brainstorming process, but let's begin with a few of my favorite exercises:

LIST THE THINGS YOU LOVE/LIST THE THINGS YOU HATE

What do you feel passionately about one way or the other? The things we love are often representative of who we are and what makes us tick—as are the things that just fire us up and make us nuts. I suggest you take out a notebook or the Notes app on your phone and spend five minutes writing down as many things as you can think of that you love, then as many things as you can think of that you hate. *(Or that mostly annoy or aggravate you; "hate" is a strong word.)* Record your everyday ruminations as you go about your daily activities. You never know what thought it could inspire in the future, so—Write. Everything. Down. What do you like to do in your spare time? Where is the place, big or small, that you feel most at home? Try to list for yourself the things that get you excited—the things you would choose to engage in or with every day if you had no other obligations. Your passions (and annoyances) can often be a helpful launching point for identifying small stories about what makes you a valuable asset in an academic or social environment.

A note: When I say "things" I am referring to everything from an object to a place to a feeling to a very specific scenario or activity. In fact, I recommend you try as hard as you can to interpret "things" loosely. Just complete the sentence "I love…" and be as specific as possible. Here are some examples:

Things Stacey Loves

World travel *(especially to Japan)*
Trying to eat an entire pizza
Being cozy
When my plants don't die
Wearing a ring on each finger
The New York Mets
Buying books even though I already own SO MANY unread books
Flower arranging
New York City street fairs
The first day of vacation
The Real Housewives of Anywhere
Modern art and architecture
Eating dinner out with my family
Eating dinner out by myself
Words and how they can impact other people

Then complete the sentence "I hate…" being as specific as possible:

Things Stacey Hates

Slow walkers in NYC
Sneezing *(I really do)*
Waiting in line
Being too cold
Being too hot
People who are rude to service people
My partner's taste in music

Doing laundry
Forgetting my glasses at home
Wearing beige
Having my iPhone ringer on
Not finishing a book I've started, even if it's boring me to tears
Obvious grammar errors
Laziness

But what do these things say about me? What might they communicate in essay form, or how can they point to a potential topic? I'm glad you asked.

Things Stacey Loves:

World travel *(especially to Japan)*

Why I love it: I've been to Japan more than thirty times, have a passion for the food/fashion/overall culture, and am finally learning the language and hoping to live there for part of the year.

What it might say about me: I'm eager to explore outside of my comfort zone and love to immerse myself in other ways of living, putting my own life and culture into perspective.

Trying to eat an entire pizza

Why I love it: I love food. Period. And I can eat more than people twice my size.

What it might say about me: I'm curious, adventurous, and willing to take a *(too)* big bite out of life.

Being cozy

Why I love it: I hate turning myself off and going to sleep, but the thought of being warm and comfy gets me there.

What it might say about me: I've learned that to calm my too-busy brain, I need rituals to help me unwind. I have a good handle on my mental and physical needs, so I know how to maintain my well-being even when I'm stressed out. *(For instance, during freshman year of college!)*

When my plants don't die

Why I love it: I became a plant mom during COVID and am proud *(and shocked?)* to have kept my babies alive for so long.

What it might say about me: I am ready for responsibility and can pour love and care into anything, even unresponsive ferns.

Wearing a ring on each finger

Why I love it: I am a chronic over-accesorizer, which I inherited from my mom. Some of my personal idols are also big baubles women: Iris Apfel, Joan Rivers, and a bunch of other (now deceased, *broken-heart emoji*) older women you young'uns probably won't know. *(But look them up!)*

What it might say about me: I'm a little extra and learned how to embrace my over-the-top-ness thanks to the unabashed women in my life.

The New York Mets

Why I love it: They've been my dad's favorite team since he was eight. I was motivated to follow them as a result, and they have been both easy and hard to love as historical underdogs.

What it might say about me: I value family and my connection with my dad, and nothing relaxes me like enjoying hot dogs together on a warm day at the ballpark. And I'm staunchly loyal to my team *(or chosen family)*, whether they win or lose.

Buying books even though I already own SO MANY unread books

Why I love it: I am an obsessive reader with a lot of interests. Reading feeds my imagination and helps me with my own writing.

What it might say about me: I'm intellectually curious and always trying to up my skill level, exploring books on a wide range of topics by authors from all around the world.

Now for a few things I hate:

Slow walkers in NYC

Why I hate it: I have a minimum speed of 1,000 miles an hour while walking. Please move.

What it might say about me: I'm a New Yorker who never stops moving and gets a lot done. My ambitions drive me at top speed to the next destination. *(Literal or metaphorical!)*

Sneezing

Why I hate it: My sneezes are full-body, convulsive affairs. *(Ouch!)*
What it might say about me: I hate being sick. I don't have the patience for it. It slows me down! *(Did I mention my insatiable drive yet?)*

Not finishing a book I've started, even if it's boring me to tears

Why I hate it: I love books and I respect authors, so even when a book isn't doing it for me, I can't stand the thought of leaving it partially unread.
What it might say about me: Once I start something, I am committed to seeing it through even when it gets tough. I also respect the efforts and opinions of others, even when I don't agree with their point of view or communication style.

Being too cold

Why I hate it: It's no fun!
What it might say about me: Not much! All of these ideas can't be winners!

Having my iPhone ringer on

Why I hate it: The sound interrupts me when I'm focused on other things.
What it might say about me: Although it's crucial to be reachable in our digital world, I like to give my full attention to the task at hand, especially if I'm with another person. I value in-person interaction and quiet focus over the quick thrill of notifications. *(Wait, was that a vibration?)*

People who are rude to service people

Why I hate it: I was once Boston's least-talented waitress *(not that I didn't try)* and was treated terribly by many.
What it might say about me: I know many jobs are harder than they look. Compassion is critical.

Wearing beige

Why I hate it: I express myself through my clothing *(see accessories above)* and I love bright colors. Beige brings me down!
What it might say about me: I'd rather stand out for being too bright and too much myself than force myself into a "beige" box just to fit in.

The point of this exercise—and many of the others I recommend—is to give you a jumping-off point for inspiration. There is nothing less inspiring than staring at a blank page, waiting for an idea to magically arrive. So trick your brain into coming up with the answer by thinking about the things you think a lot about already! Extrapolate from there.

GET ACTIVE

Step away from your keyboard. Engaging in an activity you enjoy (versus sitting at your desk in frustration) helps alleviate some of the pressure that comes along with starting the process and opens your mind to new and unexpected possibilities. Get your blood and creative juices flowing. Hop on the treadmill. Go outside. Engage in your normal daily activities. Notice things. Write things down. Open your receptors. Take a walk while you think. Eat an ice cream cone. Clear your head, observe your surroundings, let your mind drift, and feel the ideas flow in!

GO HUNTING FOR MILESTONES

Visual prompts can be immensely effective in sparking memories, pushing stories to the front of your brain, and inspiring reflection. Your house, the homes of your loved ones, your school, the locker room, and your dance studio can all be places stuffed with objects that turn on a lightbulb. Go through your phone albums or your social media feeds and brainstorm using pictures. Remember when you went to the 2015 World Series with your dad? *(You probably don't, but I do!)* Look around your bedroom. What items jump out to you as things that have meaning? Does a hand-lettered sign remind you of organizing a welcoming committee for your classmate who was returning from a lengthy stay at the hospital? Does an almost fully used watercolor set reflect the amount of time you spend making art? Do the stray socks reveal your athletic prowess or messy creative mind?

Do this exercise in any place you spend a lot of time: the bio lab, the school bus, your uncle's mechanic shop, your temple, or your favorite taco place. Try to jog your memory for the most meaningful events in your life thus far. Think about birthdays and anniversaries; special visits from long-lost friends; competitions you won (or lost). Up to this point in your life, what have been your most cherished memories and why? You might not end up writing about your seventh-grade science fair, but there could be a smaller, more significant story to mine from there, like the unexpected friendship you developed with the school janitor when you dropped your moldy bread experiment on the floor.

2. DOS AND DON'TS

While you are generating your giant rolling list of ideas, it helps to approach your deep dive with a few things in mind because some ideas are going to call out louder than others. Below is your to-do list as you sift through your idea soup.

DO

Do Embrace Narcissism

This is one of those times when we are going to encourage you to talk about yourself and only yourself. No matter what, the essay needs to be about *you*. Even if you love dinosaurs, the essay can't be about dinosaurs—it needs to be about *your* love of dinosaurs and how that has impacted *your* life choices, passions, and/or future goals. And this essay isn't about Grandma Mimi *(though I hear she is a lovely woman)*—it's about what your relationship with her taught you about yourself.

Do Dig for Details

Many students are under the false impression that the college essay should aim to tell the story of your life. But this exercise is not about stuffing every one of your important experiences into 650 words. Discriminate. Focus on one thing that is representative of your larger qualities. Look to the small moments and be specific. It is often the small details that make for the best essays; the most effective ones tell tiny stories that illustrate a larger personality trait or passion. Writing about your general passion for music is much less evocative than the story of how you washed three hundred cars in twenty days in order to send your choir to the all-state competition. Find the compelling stories within your stories. You often have a very small space in which to express yourself, which is why these essays lend themselves to bite-sized tales that are representative of the whole, instead of broad subjects that say very little in-depth about your inherent nature.

Do Get It All Down

To be truly effective, the brainstorming process has to be devoid of self-criticism and judgment. You never know which ideas are going to spark others, so as you begin to come up with topics, take notes on everything. You're not allowed to cross an idea off the list until you've squeezed your brain dry of inspiration over the course of at least three separate brainstorming sessions. Give yourself some time to cultivate and build upon your initial thoughts. The subjects that pop into your brain first are floating at the surface for a reason, even if just to lead you one step closer to your final, brilliant idea. The catalyst could be anywhere. Once you put on your observer hat, you're much more likely to notice these things.

***

So you have your pen and paper in hand and you're ready to dig into this brainstorming process. *(JK, you're on your computer checking Reddit, but close enough.)* Are there certain common brainstorming pitfalls you should watch out for as you bravely plunge forward into the dark abyss of endless ideas? You bet there are! Here are a few of the most prevalent. *(Let's try not to do these things, shall we?)*

DON'T

Don't Fail to Put in Enough Brainstorming Time

I am going to say this to you now, and I will say it to you five hundred times before the end of this book: Time is the most valuable weapon applicants can wield against the college essay! Start early and devote yourself to the process for a chunk of real, substantial time each day.

Don't Ignore Your Instincts

You know when something feels right and when something feels too risky, overdone, or boring. Trust your gut.

Don't Trash Ideas Before You Fully Explore Them

This is another thing you will hear from me more than once: Keep everything. Record all of your ideas. Do not throw anything away until you know you won't use it *(which for me is defined by the click of a submission button).*

Don't Try Too Hard to Come Up with Ideas That Are Quirky versus Authentic

Some people brainstorm for college essay topics and decide they want to compare themselves to a toaster oven. Others are inspired to write more of a straight A-to-B story. I will talk more about story structure and strategy in chapter 5, but the most important thing to keep in mind during topic generation is that it doesn't pay to be weird for weird's sake. If you are totes norm, let that totes norm flag fly; you're still awesome and not everyone naturally expresses themselves on the page in grand metaphors. Explore what comes naturally. The results will feel more authentically YOU.

Don't Rule Out Tried-and-True Topics That Could Be Powerful If Handled with Sincerity and Creativity

Not everyone has an extraordinary experience from which they can draw inspiration at age seventeen. But every seventeen-year-old can tell their average life story in new and inventive ways. Admissions officers aren't expecting you to have traveled the world, invented the cure for a rare disease, or won the national hot dog eating competition. *(Though I would truly respect you for that!)* Most applicants share a similar set of life experiences, so it's not surprising that some tried-and-true topics end up pushing their way to the surface over and over again. Still, just because a subject is oft covered does not mean it is a topic to be avoided. It's how you treat the subject matter that makes all the difference. This is why I don't believe there are any subjects that are off limits. How did this subject affect your life? What did you learn from your experiences? How has this part of your personal journey made you a better person?

Don't Fail to Find a Good Balance Between Helpful Parental Input and Parental Takeover

You can let Mom and Dad help but remember that at the end of the day this is *your* college essay. Same goes for friends, siblings, frenemies, and cats. *(Please do not let your cat choose your college essay topic for you.)*

3. NARROWING DOWN YOUR TOPICS

Let's assume you've followed all of my dos and don'ts. You're simply swimming in potential essay topics, a veritable ocean of your likes and dislikes, reflections from your walks, and inspiration drawn from objects in your room and home. Now what?

Now it's time to fish the best ideas out of those proverbial waters. Maybe you've heard of groupings of the Big Three: the Big Three automobile manufacturers (Ford, Chrysler, and General Motors), the Big Three in economics (Adam Smith, Karl Marx, and John Maynard Keynes). In college essay advising land, we have what I call the Gargantuan Four: four things that define a successful essay. Identifying the Gargantuan Four is a shortcut test to tell if an essay has a successful overarching theme and detailed messaging that will leave an admissions officer with a substantive, memorable impression.

THE GARGANTUAN FOUR

1. **Topic:** The topic is the general subject matter as defined from the ten-thousand-foot view. In half a sentence, what is your essay about? Is it about how mountain climbing with your dad taught you when to (and when not to) take risks? Or about how the food in your home city of Montreal is a metaphor for your most winning characteristics? You should be able to easily define this, and if you can't, it's possible your topic is too complicated.

Here are some possible topics based on my likes and dislikes:

- My love of over-accessorizing and how I use clothing to express myself
- How I learned to take care of plants and what I learned from it
- Why I love Japan and how that love defines me

All of these are subjects that can be expanded upon to include the other three gargantuan factors we're about to discuss.

2. **Differentiating Factor:** The differentiating factor is one of the most crucial elements of the essay. It is what sets your writing apart from other submissions. This is often known as "the hook." What grabs a reader and reels them in? Is it your killer opening line? ("I wouldn't be caught dead wearing beige.") Or your quirky format? (Journal Entry: A Day in the Life of a Plant Mom.) Maybe it's your use of metaphor (what the colors in my wardrobe represent) or a story about you that is so unique and wholly *you* that it couldn't be anyone else's. (I've been to Japan more than thirty times because I'm THAT OBSESSED.)

Here are a few helpful questions you can ask yourself to test if your topic has a built-in differentiating factor:

- What's new about the angle you're presenting?
- Are you drawing an unexpected comparison?

- Are you the only one who can tell this story?
- Does the story upend people's expectations?
- Is it stylistically distinct? Are you using a literary device?
- How will this distinguish you from other similarly qualified applicants? (For example: You're a math student who is focusing on his love of theater.)

3. **Overarching Message:** This is at the core of what a student is trying to communicate about themselves to admissions. Essentially: What is the point of the essay? Why are you telling this story? The overarching message is different from the essay topic in that it focuses on a student's perspective and objectives.

For example, some of my overarching messages might be as follows:

- I'd rather stand out for being too bright and too much myself than force myself into a "beige" box just to fit in.
- I am ready for responsibility and will pour love and care into anything, even unresponsive ferns.
- I'm eager to explore outside of my comfort zone and love to immerse myself in other ways of living, putting my own life and culture into perspective.

You'll notice that these are themes I started to identify when I made my Likes and Dislikes list. What constitutes a successful essay topic often makes its way to the surface early in the brainstorming process.

4. **Admissions Takeaway:** The purpose of the college essay is to reveal something about yourself to admissions. And that something you're hoping to reveal is your value. Why will you make a valuable addition to any campus? What are your strengths and how will they positively impact the people around you? What are your core qualities, and how will you use them to make your time in college a success?

Here's how I defined some of my qualities for the topics I've been unpacking:

- *Beige*: I am a supreme extrovert who isn't afraid to express myself. I am a chameleon without losing my sense of self. (I wear many—*literal*—hats!) My goal is to bring brightness to any occasion and lift the spirits of others.
- *Plants*: I am responsible, reliable, caring, and compassionate. I am also a person who is eager to pick up new hobbies and interests. I didn't have

a single plant before COVID, and now I have thirty *(!)*, and I naturally build community around what I love *(talking to other plant parents)*.

- *Japan*: I am intellectually curious and when I'm interested in something I dive deep. My appetite for new experiences is insatiable. I know that no matter how much I come to know about Japan, there will always be more to learn. And that is exciting for me.

Yes, I have already been to college, but I still hope these are qualities that would make an admissions officer want to add me to their campus.

Your challenge is to find an approach that contains all of the Gargantuan Four. If one of these elements is missing from your idea, you either need to rework the subject in question or throw it in the discard pile. But as you go through the brainstorming exercises I detailed above, fruitful G4-filled ideas will eventually flood your brain—I promise.

But as You Start to Narrow Down Your Ideas, How Will You Know When You've Found the Winning Topic?

You no longer want to hurl large objects across the room.

You can breathe again.

You're excited to start writing. *(Yes, it happens.)*

No, seriously. When you find the right topic, you know it. All of a sudden, the pressure of writing a perfectly compelling college essay lifts a little. *(Not completely—that would be a miracle!)*

Ultimately, students who write effective college essays aren't worrying about what admissions wants to hear. They are thinking about how to best express themselves and what a near-stranger might want to know to feel better acquainted with them.

Finally, when you've isolated a subject you think will represent you well, do a quick test to see how you can back it into a prompt. For example, if you're planning to write about how your classmate had a different opinion during a discussion about the impact of school walkouts, read through the prompts quickly to see where your essay might fit. You could use this topic as a response to "challeng[ing] your beliefs" or "something…that made you thankful in a surprising way." All of a sudden you will realize that—WHOA!—that car ride with your mom was totally a "period of personal growth."

DUH TIP: BRAINSTORMING IS A GROUP SPORT

Sometimes advice is hardest to take from the people who are closest to you. And I know more than anyone how some adults like to stick their noses into this admissions business and overexert their influence. That said, your parents remember things about your past seventeen years on this earth that you may not. Weirdly, they're paying attention. So are your best friends, siblings, and teachers. Talking to people who are close to you at this stage of the game is essential. Essay writing doesn't have to occur on an island.

4 How Do You Conquer the Blank Page? Freewriting Your Face Off

Congratulations! If you've made it to this chapter, you have probably identified a topic so perfect that it makes you weep with joy. Or you have a story or idea in mind that you're *pretty* sure will showcase some of your best personal qualities while communicating something admissions doesn't already know about you and you're not exactly elated to the point of *sobbing*, but you're also no longer crying in frustration *(which is also a really good place to start)*.

Whatever the case, it's time to turn one of the magical ideas you Backwards Brainstormed into a giant pile of related words, phrases, sentences—even paragraphs! And the way I recommend you do this is through one of my very favorite phases of the Uncommon College Essay Approach: the time-tested practice of Freewriting Your Face Off.

One of the greatest misconceptions applicants have about the college essay *(and about writing in general)* is that ideas are supposed to spill out of your brain and onto the page, perfectly formed on the first try. *(If only!)* In my own writing, this is almost never how it works. In fact, you're currently reading a paragraph I revisited and massaged at least a handful of times before I released it into the world to meet your beautiful eyeballs. As with so many creative pursuits, starting with some broad, messy strokes followed by thoughtful refinement is often the most effective, least stress-inducing path to generating a masterpiece. It's possible that the Declaration of Independence underwent a little revision before John Hancock put his John Hancock on it. And maybe, just maybe, Michelangelo didn't paint the Sistine Chapel in one sitting. Following this logic, you will likely need to swim in a little word soup on your way to crafting a college admissions essay that captures your ideal story, message, and tone. And I'm going to teach you how to do it with a sense of freedom and abandon that results in creative and insightful writing, while allowing you to—dare I suggest—enjoy yourself along the way.

HOW TO SET THE MOOD

I'm certain you've mastered the daily multitasking required to answer texts, scour your social media feeds, watch an endless stream of YouTube videos, and pen the most stunning personal essay in history *all at the same time*, but this is one occasion for which it is critical to escape your everyday distractions and focus. Your writing environment sets the stage for success, so before you sit down to write:

Disconnect

Check your email, catch up on the group chat, and then cut the cord. *(I know you're wireless—say hello to metaphor!)* Cutting yourself off from the internet and all related distractions almost instantly sharpens your concentration and unlocks creativity. *(It also illuminates how much we compulsively engage with technology—just count how many times you check your phone even when it's on airplane mode.)* If you don't trust yourself to disconnect from Wi-Fi and stay off, try using software that locks you out of your internet connection for a set period of time. Have your little sister hide your phone from you for an hour if she's the kind of sister who will eventually give it back to you. Do whatever you have to do. You can text your BFFAEAE *(that's how millennials say bestie)* in an hour or two when you take a regularly scheduled internet break. *(I'm trying to help you focus, not torment you forever!)*

Find Your Happy Place

Some students have luck working at the local library. Others need the quiet of their rooms to be truly productive. A few might do their best work on airplanes where they are otherwise unreachable. *(Though this seems like an expensive and generally unsustainable coworking space.)* Or you could be one of those people who is inspired by noisy coffee shops and light people-watching, and that's fine, too. Know thyself. Before you get to work, identify a chair, classroom, café, or picnic table that will provide the space and setting you prefer and go to there.

Compartmentalize Your Fears

Maybe you don't think you can write a stellar college admissions essay. And why would you? You've likely never done it before! This may be your first time writing a personal essay of any kind, but every day you churn out hundreds *(thousands? millions?)* of texts, dash off emails, tell multi-part stories, and express bold opinions. You have the experience to condense and communicate your beliefs, values, interests, and passions; you just don't know it yet. It may sound corny, but positive thinking can be so powerful when facing a new challenge. Repeat the "I cans" to yourself and abolish "I can't" from your vocabulary. Yes, you *can* write this admissions essay. Yes, you *can* finish an entire pizza in one sitting. *(I am proof that this mantra works.)* Perspective is everything, and the right attitude goes a long way.

Get Inspired—But Not from the Sources You'd Expect

This will not be the last time I mention this, but poring over dozens of sample college admissions essays immediately before sitting down to write your own can be a debilitating exercise. I understand the instinct to research the assignment to try to internalize what has worked for students in the past. Still, I will forever try to dissuade applicants from looking at too many—often any—college essay samples or examples. I'll dig into why reading other applicants' essays can be a hindrance in chapter 10. What is important now is that you know where to look for inspiration. I recommend thumbing through personal essay collections that don't focus on admissions. Joan Didion, Melissa Febos, Leslie Jamison, George Saunders, and David Sedaris are just a few modern masters of the craft. Comb through your favorite websites and bookmark opinion pieces that might interest you. Before you start to write your own story, get a sense of how first-person essays are constructed. Gather clues about how to tell your story in unexpected ways. *(Maybe start at the end of the story?)* There are infinite ways to write a personal essay; give yourself the opportunity to peruse a few without the baggage of comparison. Gather your brainstorming notes, choose what you believe is your Winning Topic, and open a fresh document *(or page, if you're old school)*. Now you're ready to write.

WHAT IS FREEWRITING?

Mark Twain said, "The secret to getting ahead is getting started." E. L. Doctorow said, "Writing is an exploration. You start from nothing and learn as you go." And word wizard Stacey Brook still says, "The blank page is your enemy. Conquer it with words."

Freewriting is, at its core, just as it sounds: the act of writing freely. It is the exercise of jotting down whatever comes to mind, without judgment or consideration of the final product. Its purpose is to encourage you to record your stream-of-consciousness thoughts on the page, while training you to trust your gut and write your brains out *(or trust your brain and write your guts out)*. Those ideas you brainstormed and narrowed down in chapter 3 rose to the top for a reason, so roll with the momentum they bring. I cannot emphasize this enough: Don't stress. Just write.

This step in the essay-writing process, which feels the messiest, is also the step that sets you up for future glory. A blank page can be terrifying, so your job is simply to un-blankify it. Now is not the time for judgment. *(Just like you're not judging the new word I just came up with.)* Now is the time to spit it all out, record every detail, follow every tangent. The deeper you dig, the greater your chance of unearthing the hidden gems buried in the deepest layers of your memory. Your stories, complex metaphors, and series of anecdotes are all in your noggin, but the components may be scattered. Bring all of those thoughts—in whatever form they appear—to the page where you can analyze them. Later. Initially it can be hard to distinguish writing of value from the discards, so keep everything *(I mean it!)* and keep going. The more you write, the more you will have to choose from when you begin to pull together a cohesive draft. Record all of your wildest and most random ideas because at the end of the day, even diamonds need to be cut.

A glorious side effect of Freewriting Your Face Off is that it helps you build up what I like to think of as college essay endurance. The brain is a muscle and storytelling is a skill that doesn't turn on with the flip of a switch. The more you exercise this function of your brain, the smoother it will operate.

DRILL AROUND, DRILL DOWN

One of the largest misconceptions about freewriting is that your efforts should be focused on covering a wide breadth of material, without digging too deep into any one subject. Or that you should mine down to the core of a few specific elements of your story, focusing on uncovering small details related to very specific pathways without exploring the larger picture. But the most effective freewrites cover *both* aspects, the breadth and the depth, which is why I encourage you to both drill around and drill down.

First, think about your topic in all its majestic glory. What possible anecdotes might be included in your explorations of that topic? If you are an engineer who once attended an inventors' fair with your older brother, what led you to that event? How long have you been interested in making things? What are some of your favorite creations, and how did you come up with each idea? What final lessons might you learn or conclusions might you draw based on your interest in invention? Jot down some notes on each of these subjects, leaving space to fill in details later. This is what I call the "Drill Around."

Once you have raked out some glittery potential ideas, it's time to take the jackhammer and transition to "Drilling Down." Follow your most promising ideas and interesting tangents as far as they will go. If you are our engineer friend, choose your favorite invention. Maybe it was a dog-washing robot. *(Wishful thinking!)* Where did the idea for this creation come from? How long did it take you to plan out your project, and did anyone help you along the way? Where did you get the parts to build your creation? What other challenges did you experience? Dive into each subject headfirst, recording every detail you can think of. Nothing is too minute or too unimportant to get down. Forget minimalism. MORE IS MORE.

It may feel like you're veering off course as you delve into a sidenote to your main story, but these divergences are often the source of unexpected and compelling details. Following your train of thought about your grandfather's immigration experience could lead to a memory of a childhood book about underwater animals that taught you how to speak English. Be as descriptive as you can, and don't worry about overdoing it. You can always scrap what doesn't work.

***

What if you start drilling around and down for golden nuggets and you immediately hit a wall? Here are a few guidelines to help you effectively execute your excavation:

THE RULES OF FREEWRITING

Just Write

Even if you're not in the mood, even if you don't think you'll like what's coming out on the page, even if you hate everything you're writing that day—Just. Freaking. Write. If your thoughts don't come out the way you want them to, make a small notation using asterisks or bolding that indicates you may want to circle back and revise. If you don't know what to write about, start jotting down a description of your day. Just don't stop the forward motion. At this phase in the process, bad writing is not your enemy. *(Your enemy is the blank page.)*

Don't Write

Maybe writing isn't your favorite way to express yourself. Perhaps you're more of a visual artist or you feel more comfortable talking through your ideas. When getting words down on the page feels unnatural, don't forgo the freewrite—go around it! If you suddenly feel the urge to draw, sketch it out. Make a diagram or an idea map. If you think you're a better conversationalist than a writer, record yourself telling your story to a friend and then transcribe your best ideas. You can even describe your ideas to a few different people to note which elements appear over and over again. *(Those could be important!)* Do whatever it takes to keep telling your story.

Forget Spelling and Grammar (For Now)

Attention to details like grammar and spelling is essential to the final draft of your essay. But now is not the time to be overly fussy. Don't stop your flow to check the spelling of "Massachusetts" or look up the rules for dangling modifiers. You don't even have to write in fully fleshed-out paragraphs if they aren't coming naturally in the moment. For now, we give you license not to care. *(Though please, for the love of English teachers around the world, try to use "your" and "you're" correctly.)*

No Judgment

You are absolutely not allowed to judge your first attempts. No backtracking. Do not reread the sentence you just wrote to see if you like it. *(I still mean it!)* Don't think about whether or not you're going in the right direction. Don't look back. Just keep swimming. *(Don't stop believin'!)* Just. Freaking. Write. Or draw. Or talk. Interpretive dance if you prefer. Only you know the best way to get your thoughts out of your brain and into the world.

Solicit Prompts

This is one of my favorite tricks. Tell a mentor or family member you trust about your topic and ask them to assign you a set of interview questions. If this person read an essay about your topic, written by you, what would they want to know? Freewriting in response to bite-sized prompts is a great way to inspire a new flood of ideas and break through initial freewriting trepidation. Make sure to request that whoever asks you these questions challenges you to dig for details. You are trying to tell a vivid story that stays interesting for the length of an entire essay. If, for example, you're writing about your journey through the intimidating world of improv comedy, maybe your mom will ask you about your scariest attempt at coming up with an idea off the cuff. Perhaps she'll ask you what random character you enjoyed playing the most and how you decide what kinds of details you will try to bring into a new scene. Why is improv scarier than a presentation at the front of the classroom? Getting a new perspective in the mix will pose many questions you may not have thought to ask yourself.

ADVICE IN ACTION: SOLICITING PROMPTS/FREEWRITING

I asked one part of my brain *(the essay advising part)* to come up with prompts for another part of my brain *(the part I assigned the task of freewriting for a personal statement just for fun—NERD!)* to show you what some freewrites in response to solicited prompts might look like for my "Plant Mom" topic. These exercises are by no means comprehensive; I could—and would—assign myself more rounds of questions based on these responses in preparation for writing a personal statement.

Now, as you look over my freewrites below, consider the following: Is everything I have typed interesting enough to be included in a final essay? Most definitely not! Was I allowed to judge whether I liked what I was writing while I was writing it? You know I wasn't! The point of freewriting exercises is to give yourself a safe space for rambling, experimentation, and *(likely)* the creation of some unexpected genius. So enjoy my stream-of-consciousness thinking, my notes to myself, my jokes that only I will get. These freewrites are being presented in their unedited, unjudged form. I have to follow the rules I ask everyone else to follow, after all!

Plant Mom Prompts

1. **When did you buy your first plant and why? What kind of plant was it? Why were you drawn to it?**

   I have owned (and killed) multiple orchids in the past—most of them gifted to me. And I have had a life-sized replica of a mid-sized Audrey 2 (from *Little Shop of Horrors*) on my windowsill that I once commissioned for an obnoxiously authentic Halloween costume. But the first plant I ever bought I purchased while in lockdown during COVID. Perhaps it was because I was lonely or bored or both? My first leafy plant purchase was a snake plant that came to me pre-potted in a short, gold ceramic pot. It was planted using a material called coir (made of coconut husk) instead of potting soil, which kept things extra light and neat. I decided on a snake plant because the internet said they were virtually impossible to kill, and I had little faith in my tending skills at the time. The care instructions were easy enough to follow. Water, put on a sunny windowsill, ignore, repeat. I figured I could handle that!

2. **Why didn't you think you were someone who could keep a plant alive in the past? Was there any actual evidence this might be the case?**

I didn't have pets growing up. My parents got our first family dog about fourteen seconds after I left for college, which definitely didn't make me feel like they immediately moved on. (This is sarcasm in case it's hard to tell.) Any pets we had in the Brook home were tiny, usually won at a carnival and short-lived. I don't think a goldfish made it past day 2 in our house, even when my father made a true effort to extend its life by buying a real tank with a filtration system and some plastic coral to inspire it to live longer. My little brother brought home hermit crabs from a school fair once, which stunk up the house and disappeared swiftly and under mysterious circumstances. We had a couple of giant fake plants around the house because I grew up in the '80s when everything big and fake was embraced. My father did love to landscape and work on the flowers around the house, but there were never any flowers *in* the house. My mother notoriously hates flowers ("they just die!"), so the lucky man never had to pay for roses on Valentine's Day.

3. **In retrospect, were there any indications you might actually have a green thumb? What were they?**

My father did love to garden, and my siblings and I really liked helping him plant in the spring. We all especially loved lantanas, a flowering plant that comes in a kaleidoscopic range of color variations, many of them super pigmented (think magentas, deep oranges, vivid yellows). I also discovered I loved cut flowers in my adulthood (sorry, Mom). The streets of New York City are filled with them, as they're a constant presence in the city's bodegas, and I often fill my home with tulips and spray roses and whatever other flowers are in season. I also started taking Japanese flower arranging (called ikebana) lessons a few years before the pandemic, which taught me some fascinating tricks/strategies for making flowers last longer. (Use a toothpick to prick a hole through the stem near the top of a tulip head and/or put a penny in the water and the stems will stay more rigid and upright for longer!)

4. **Why do you think you bought so many plants in such a short period of time?**

I have always been a collector of things (my nice way to describe hoarding), and once I become fixated on something, I often go ALL THE WAY IN. After I bought the snake plant I decided to experiment with a few succulents as well, as they're also known for being hardy and fairly difficult to kill. I soon discovered that I could buy plants online without their permanent pots and search for ceramics (another one of my loves/collection obsessions) to hold them, which launched a multi-week project of cultivating the perfect collection of interestingly potted succulents on my windowsill. As they often do for me, things quickly got out of hand, and I soon had a collection of fourteen succulents on my hands. Luckily, I have a giant windowsill that gets a lot of sun. When those didn't die, I got a bit braver and bought two more leafy plants, a monstera plant and a money tree. I love them both dearly, but I also regret buying the money tree because I am deeply superstitious that if it dies, I will lose my life savings. What a relaxing hobby I have!

5. **What does your current plant care routine look like? How long does it take? What is the hardest part? What is the most enjoyable part?**

Honestly, plant care for the plants I own is super easy—otherwise I don't think I would have made it this far. I water my leafy plants once a week during the warmer months, twice during the colder months. For the monstera and the money tree, they're so big now that I have to lift with my knees to get the pots off the ground and lean them into my kitchen sink so I can soak the soil and let the excess water leave through the drainage hole. I water the succulents every two to four weeks, rotating them into and out of the kitchen sink two at a time.

Two years ago my money tree was looking a little unwell (OH, NO) and the internet suggested that it perhaps was becoming "root bound," meaning its container was getting too small, causing the roots to tangle and prevent water absorption. In one of the most stressful tasks of my life, I put painter's tarp on the floor of my NYC apartment and repotted both of my big plants. I've never been so nervous to get something right. Also, repotting plants indoors is a hell of an undertaking. Would not recommend! But both of my children came through and they are so much healthier and happier with room to expand!

6. **Why do your plants feel like "plant babies?" In what ways do you anthropomorphize them, and why do you think you do this?**

First of all, they are alive! Duh. But mostly I think of them as keeping me company. They surround me all day and bring a lot of light and energy into my world. Living in the city with no personal outdoor space, I love having green so close to me. And I do care deeply whether these plants live or die. I don't have a 100% success rate—every once in a while I will neglect a succulent too much while traveling or something I can't identify will go wrong. I think I've lost three or four plants since the pandemic. And they're not actual children, so I get over it. I also don't name my plants. But I do clean their leaves carefully and think about whether or not they are getting the nutrition they need and look at them lovingly and often.

7. **How is the process of taking care of plants therapeutic? What other benefits might it have?**

   There is something so soothing about watching something grow and thrive. I particularly love removing dried leaves (a natural part of the tending process), because it makes me feel like I am removing extraneous elements so the healthy ones can grow even bigger and stronger. I also think exposure to nature—even "manicured nature" as I often call it—is healthy.

8. **How else is this tendency to nurture represented in your life? Where else might Plant Mom Stacey show up in the world?**

   I do love taking care of other people and my love languages abound. Tending to plants probably corresponds most to "acts of service" and I know people I love appreciate when I do something that helps make their lives easier, even if it's small—like picking up an extra milk on the way home for my mom. I am a pretty responsible person by nature, but taking care of plants has reinforced my desire to be responsible to others, which is very rewarding, I find. Plants also represent chosen family for me in a way. I choose and love to be responsible to them. I feel very similarly about my college essay students every year. I love working with them, it is something I choose to do enthusiastically each year, and each student feels like part of my family by the end of the process.

FINDING PATTERNS AND PLUCKING GEMS

Once you have thoroughly excavated your brain and mined your memory, how do you decide which elements belong in your personal essay? What separates the good from the bad? Mostly, it comes down to finding the big patterns and plucking the small gems.

Finding Big Patterns

When you begin to dig into your freewrites, the first thing you want to do is look for overlap in content. What themes come up repeatedly? (Like the lack of living things—other than people—in my childhood home.) Is there a specific challenge you describe multiple times? Do you find yourself writing about a few different aspects of the same small event? (Like gardening with my dad.) Is there a metaphor that repeats itself in various incarnations? Look for the interplay between the answers to questions posed by your freewrite interviewer. How do your responses play off each other? (Did what start as a random activity to fill time become a regular means of self-care/caring for others?) Highlight anything that feels important. I'm not being metaphorical here—*physically* highlight the patterns in your document using the highlight tool or an actual neon yellow marker, if you're one of those retro types. (You can also use the bold function as I do below if highlighting is unavailable to you.) Use another color (or your underline function) for the next step in the process.

Once you start to identify the patterns in your thought processes you will likely realize that, without even trying, your story is already leading you in a natural direction.

For example, here I've used bolded text for parts of my freewrites because they show some recurring themes:

1. **Why didn't you think you were someone who could keep a plant alive in the past? Was there any actual evidence this might be the case?**

   I didn't have pets growing up. My parents got our first family dog about fourteen seconds after I left for college, which definitely didn't make me feel like they immediately moved on. (This is sarcasm in case it's hard to tell.) **Any pets we had in the Brook home were tiny, usually won at a carnival and short-lived. I don't think a goldfish made it past day 2 in our house, even when my father made a true effort to extend its life by buying a real tank with a filtration system and some plastic coral to inspire it to live longer.** My little brother brought home hermit crabs from a school fair once, which stunk up the house and disappeared swiftly and under mysterious circumstances. We had a couple of giant fake plants around the house because I grew up in the '80s when everything big and fake was embraced. **My father did love to landscape and work on the flowers around the house,** but there were never any flowers *in* the house. My mother notoriously hates flowers ("they just die!"), so the lucky man never had to pay for roses on Valentine's Day.

The bolded text in the excerpts all connect to the idea of me not believing I was a plant person as well as the initial hints that a green thumb might have been introduced by my dad.

3. **In retrospect, were there any indications you might actually have a green thumb? What were they?**

   My father did love to garden, and my siblings and I really liked helping him plant in the spring. We all especially loved lantanas, a flowering plant that comes in a kaleidoscopic range of color variations, many of them super pigmented (think magentas, deep oranges, vivid yellows). I also discovered I loved cut flowers in my adulthood (sorry, Mom). The streets of New York City are filled with them, as they're a constant presence in the city's bodegas, and **I often fill my home with tulips and spray roses and whatever other flowers are in season. I also started taking Japanese flower arranging (called ikebana) lessons a few years before the pandemic,** which taught me some fascinating tricks/strategies for making flowers last longer. (Use a toothpick to prick a hole through the stem near the top of a tulip head and/or put a penny in the water and the stems will stay more rigid and upright for longer!)

Again, I'm pulling sections showing that my love of plants might be passed down (from Dad), as well as some examples of being drawn to flowers in adulthood.

Plucking the Gems

Next, it's time to scope out the gems. Sure, it's important to identify the big picture and direction of your essay, but effective storytelling is often about the power of small moments, and the details you identify in your freewrites will help bring your story to life. The description of your mother's hands or the sound of the ignition the first time you drove a car are often the kind of details that will stick with your reader. Make these phrases and descriptions easily identifiable using your second highlight color or underline. (I've used an underline here.) Mine your freewrites for the descriptions that sing, the sentences you instantly fall in love with, the chunks of writing that actually make you proud upon first read. While much freewriting results in unusable gobbledygook, the process is bound to produce a few sparkling phrases, and many more that could ultimately shine like diamonds with a little polishing. I bet you find more gems to covet than you initially expect.

1. **Why didn't you think you were someone who could keep a plant alive in the past? Was there any actual evidence this might be the case?**

   I didn't have pets growing up. My parents got our first family dog about fourteen seconds after I left for college, which definitely didn't make me feel like they immediately moved on. (This is sarcasm in case it's hard to tell.) **Any pets we had in the Brook home were tiny, usually won at a carnival and short-lived.** I don't think a goldfish made it past day 2 in our house, even when my father made a true effort to extend its life by buying a real tank with a filtration system and some plastic coral to inspire it to live longer. My little brother brought home hermit crabs from a school fair once, which stunk up the house and disappeared swiftly and under mysterious circumstances. We had a couple of giant fake plants around the house because I grew up in the '80s when everything big and fake was embraced. **My father did love to landscape and work on the flowers around the house**, but there were never any flowers *in* the house. <u>My mother notoriously hates flowers ("they just die!"), so the lucky man never had to pay for roses on Valentine's Day.</u>

I particularly love the humor in these two "gem" lines and will almost definitely want to include them in the essay.

3. **In retrospect, were there any indications you might actually have a greenthumb? What were they?**

My father did love to garden, and my siblings and I really liked helping him plant in the spring. <u>We all especially loved lantanas, a flowering plant that comes in a kaleidoscopic range of color variations, many of them super pigmented (think magentas, deep oranges, vivid yellows).</u> I also discovered I loved cut flowers in my adulthood (sorry, Mom). The streets of New York City are filled with them, as they're a constant presence in the city's bodegas, and **I often fill my home with tulips and spray roses and whatever other flowers are in season. I also started taking Japanese flower arranging (called ikebana) lessons a few years before the pandemic**, which taught me some fascinating tricks/strategies for making flowers last longer. (Use a toothpick to prick a hole through the stem near the top of a tulip head and/or put a penny in the water and the stems will stay more rigid and upright for longer!)

This detailed description of gardening with my siblings stood out to me as something that might help really bring my essay to life. *(Spoiler alert: I end up cutting the sentence underlined above significantly in later drafts, but that's okay! This is the time to follow your initial instincts; you can always make changes and cuts down the road.)*

PRO TIP: Identify the Highlights, but Delete Nothing

Try not to review your freewrites to start wrangling your best work until you have at least double the number of words required by the prompt. You're going to want an overabundance of material to consider as you identify the best of your thoughts and words; it's much easier to snip and trim an essay that is too long than it is to add to one that isn't fully fleshed out. When you do begin to review and isolate your best efforts, always save a copy of your initial freewrites. Don't trash your extra words for good. *(I promise if you do you will regret it—and this is what the cloud is for!)* Writing the college essay is stressful enough; you don't want to have to do the digital version of dumpster diving for former drafts. Keep an initial copy of all of your freewrites saved in an easily accessible document or folder. They might even be useful for brainstorming ideas for your supplemental essays *(foreshadowing for chapter 7!)*.

OUTLINING/ESSAY MAPPING IS YOUR FRIEND

Let's assume that by now you have drilled and drilled until your fingers could tap no more and your head was verifiably empty. You have thousands of words on the page, and you have color-coded (or underlined) your best material for building out the big picture and filling in the meaningful details. Now what? Like any great adventurer with their eye on the prize, you're going to find a map to follow. *(Actually, you're going to create one for yourself out of thin air, because you're a freaking magician.)* Laying out a simple outline will make it easier to see the full trajectory of your story. It will identify holes that need to be filled and story points that need further development. Crafting an outline at this stage of the game will also help verify you have chosen a topic that is strong enough to support an entire essay. Not to mention that the outline will help establish a logical flow to ensure that admissions officers remember your most important points.

I don't believe you need to make a super detailed, fifteen-page-long catalog to chart your path forward *(though feel free to go that route if it makes you feel more organized)*. Slapping together a lightning fast, sixteen-line, broad-stroke guide to your new master plan will do just fine. And all that needs to go into this broad sketch are "Big Picture Headers" and "Supporting Subtopics" for each paragraph. You should have a pretty good idea of what these big picture themes and supports will be by now, as they've been rolling around in your brain during brainstorming and freewriting.

And if you put enough time into your freewrites, your illuminating details should be pretty easy to fill in.

ADVICE IN ACTION: BROAD-STROKES OUTLINE AND ESSAY MAP

I. I used to think I was only capable of taking care of fake plants or dead ones; I likely thought this because of my history of trying to take care of living things

- a. Audrey 2
  - b. The expired orchids
  - c. My childhood pets
  - d. My first plants

II. During COVID, out of boredom and a desire for company, I bought a plant, which quickly turned into a collection
  - a. Buying the snake plant (unlikely to die)
  - b. Adding succulents
  - c. Collecting pots and cultivating my dream indoor garden
  - d. Expanding to more leafy plants when I became more confident

III. Why I ended up being good at tending to plants and what it brought me
  - a. Love flowers and had a bit of an unrecognized green thumb already
  - b. Connected me to nature in an urban landscape
  - c. Gave me a sense of something to care for and nurture, which was rewarding
  - d. Showed me that new skills are learnable with time and effort

IV. Plants are my babies, my chosen family
  - a. I am their mom and I care for them; I love them and choose to do this
  - b. These tendencies carry over to the people I love
  - c. Even to my job with my students
  - d. Concluding sentence TBD!

Just because you make an outline doesn't mean your plan won't change; in fact, I expect a bit of tweaking as you explore potential story structures and framing devices in the next chapter. Still, following a trail that you adjust along the way is much easier than selecting from an amorphous cloud of ideas—even your best ones. Good storytelling is a function of a great idea, excellent planning, and thoughtful story flow (which I will cover in the next chapter). It is always easier to navigate your way to a story with a roadmap in front of you.

Once you have a pile of freewrites and a thoughtfully constructed outline on your hands, it's time to explore some storytelling strategies and pull together the first draft of your *(amazing)* personal essay. But for now, have another cookie—you are a freewriting expert!

5 How Do You Capture—and Keep!—a Reader's Attention? Sculpting Your Story

So you have five fistfuls of freewrites and a quickie outline burning a hole in your computer and you're thinking, "Mining for gems and organizing my thoughts was fun and all, but how do I pull my best ideas together into a story with a defined structure, an effortless flow, and a pointed purpose? And how can I tell a tale that will grab admissions officers and keep them hooked from my first word to my last?"

It's not as difficult as you might think. Believe it or not, you have some storytelling tools under your belt already. And the rest, I'm going to show you.

To start off, let's take a look at the arrows you've added to your quiver thus far. You have a killer topic, meant to slay an admissions officer with its incisive observations, ruthless wit, and deadly sincerity. You have a briefcase full of freewrites, carefully cultivated and just begging to fill up an essay page. You have an outline that you've started to fill out with the gems from your freewrites. Still, how do you use these components to craft a structured and compelling story?

WHAT DO YOU DO WITH THOSE FREEWRITES?

It's time to put your prolific freewrites in their place with the Uncommon College Essay Approach's third step: Sculpting Your Story. Open a new document and see if you can create a loose draft, plucking your highlighted sentences and rearranging them into an order that generally aligns with your outline.

Recall the beginning of my "Plant Mom" outline:

I. I used to think I was only capable of taking care of fake plants or dead ones; I likely thought this because of my history of trying to take care of living things

     a. Audrey 2

     b. The expired orchids

     c. My childhood pets

     d. My first plants

  II. During COVID, out of boredom and a desire for company, I bought a plant, which quickly turned into a collection

     a. Buying the snake plant (unlikely to die)

     b. Adding succulents

     c. Collecting pots and cultivating my dream indoor garden

     d. Expanding to more leafy plants when I became more confident

Now, let's take my headers and couple them with related freewrites:

I used to think I was only capable of taking care of fake plants or dead ones; I likely thought this because of my history of trying to take care of living things

I have owned (and killed) multiple orchids in the past—most of them gifted to me. And I have had a life-sized replica of a mid-sized Audrey 2 (from *Little Shop of Horrors*) on my windowsill that I once commissioned for an obnoxiously authentic Halloween costume.

Any pets we had in the Brook home were tiny, usually won at a carnival and short-lived. I don't think a goldfish made it past day two in our house, even when my father made a true effort to extend its life by buying a real tank with a filtration system and some plastic coral to inspire it to live longer. My little brother brought home hermit crabs from a school fair once, which stunk up the house and disappeared swiftly and under mysterious circumstances.

During COVID, out of boredom and a desire for company, I bought a plant, which quickly turned into a collection

The first plant I ever bought I purchased while in lockdown during COVID. Perhaps it was because I was lonely or bored or both? My first leafy plant purchase was a snake plant that came to me pre-potted in a short, gold ceramic pot.

I have always been a collector of things (my nice way to describe hoarding), and once I become fixated on something, I often go ALL THE WAY IN. After I bought the snake plant I decided to experiment with a few succulents as well, as they're also known for being hardy and fairly difficult to kill. I soon discovered that I could buy plants online without their permanent pots and search for ceramics (another one of my loves/collection obsessions) to hold them, which launched a multi-week project of cultivating the perfect collection of interestingly potted succulents on my windowsill. As they often do for me, things quickly got out of hand, and I soon had a collection of fourteen succulents on my hands.

***

And on and on it goes. Notice, I am not writing new material but rather plucking chunks from my freewrites and arranging them in a loose formation under relevant topic sentences. This "found draft" is essentially an expanded outline, using the best of what you've written thus far. You may have just tricked yourself into writing the core of your essay.

Now, let's start sculpting and molding the finer details. Start by following these three actions:

Snip

If you don't like what a line says about you, cut it. If it doesn't further the point of your story, say sayonara. If it's confusing or puts you to sleep, wake yourself up with a few sharp taps on the delete key. You may also love an idea that you had trouble expressing during your earlier freewrites; if you're not ready to cut it, hold that thought because you'll have another chance to expand and rewrite later on.

Flip

As you sculpt your story, some elements might not fit with your adapting plot points and story plan *(so you snip 'em!)*, and others might come in handy in ways you never expected. Maybe there are lines in your draft that are valuable, but would be better suited in a different sequence. Perhaps your planned ending paragraph should be your opener instead. Don't be shy—move things around. Experiment. You can always hit the undo button.

Fill

Search for holes in logic. Mark places where you might need to fill in crucial details. Revisit the paragraphs that contained ideas you liked, but perhaps writing you weren't in love with, and try to breathe some new life into those lines. Draft new content as you feel inspired.

The process of *snipping* away what doesn't serve the essay well, *flipping* plot points into their proper place, and *filling* in the missing details will bring you to a nice loose draft that incorporates the best elements of your outline and freewrites. But as you wield those cut, paste, and delete keys, how can you make sure you're headed toward a structure that makes sense and fully emphasizes the point you're trying to make?

ADVICE IN ACTION: COMPOSING A LOOSE PLANT MOM DRAFT

As you might have guessed by now, I took my freewrites from chapter 4 and constructed a full draft essay from them! It's important to me that you see this college essay-writing process is not theoretical—it actually works in practice. In fact, I just did it! The below 851-word draft is a compilation of my freewrites, ordered to form a coherent narrative. You'll see my story is beginning to take shape. I'm choosing the anecdotes and details that feel important to include, filling in areas that feel bare, and starting to revise sections that need to be condensed. Notice, there is still much room for cutting, tightening, and overall improvement. What I am attempting to lock in during this loose drafting process is a story order and general sense of what is important for me to communicate to the reader.

Behold, a draft that is on its way but definitely needs more work. I have marked a few places where I have snipped, flipped, and filled *(though I have done this in many places throughout the text)* so you can see how those processes look in practice. I did a fair amount of filling, especially toward the end of the essay, which isn't uncommon. Once the themes become clear, it helps to add reflection that really focuses on your desired message. I know this new information will be pared down in the final draft, but in this phase, it helps me to explore varied paths to my core sentiments.

LOOSE DRAFT

The only plants I owned before 2019 are now dead or were never alive to begin with. I half-heartedly attempted to nurture multiple orchids in my twenties, ultimately neglecting them to usher in their ultimate demise. A creepy, lifelike replica of a mid-sized Audrey 2, the talking, people-eating plant from *Little Shop of Horrors*, still sits on my windowsill, the result of an Etsy commission for an obsessively authentic Halloween costume. But my knack for helping plants thrive didn't come until I was stuck inside during the pandemic, searching for a distraction in which my attention and affection could take root. My first leafy plant purchase was a snake plant, pre-potted in a short, gold ceramic pot, which the internet said would be virtually impossible to kill. The care instructions were easy enough to follow. Water, put on a sunny windowsill, ignore, repeat. *(I have snipped and flipped quite a few lines in this section to try and achieve vivid, opening paragraph energy, though I feel at this phase I still have more refining to do, especially with the opening line.)*

Before my pandemic plant adoption, I long had a sense that I wasn't a plant person. The only living things brought into my house as a child were goldfish, usually won at a carnival and "sent to the farm upstate" within days. There were no real indoor plants, just a few clusters of the fake Anthuriums that were so popular in the '80s. My mother notoriously hates cut flowers ("they just die!"), so a bouquet of fresh tulips never decorated our kitchen table. *(I cut this section down quite a bit from my freewrites. I want admissions to get a sense of my history with plants here, but this is also background information, so I felt I needed to make these points and descriptions more concise.)*

My father did love to garden, however, and this is where my green thumb likely started to bloom, though I didn't realize it at the time. My siblings and I helped him plant outside the house every spring, bonding while sprinkling the beds with lantanas, a flowering plant that comes in a kaleidoscopic range of hyper-pigmented colors (think magentas, deep oranges, vivid yellows). I also discovered I loved cut flowers in my adulthood (sorry, Mom) and started taking lessons on Japanese flower arranging, known as ikebana, in the mid-2010s. This is where my knowledge of and facility with flowers truly germinated and flourished.

I missed the calming practice of ikebana during COVID, but flowers were hard to come by, so a snake plant had to do. My new green acquisition had been thriving for mere weeks when I decided to adopt the rest of my plant family. I have always been a collector of things, and once I become fixated on something, I often go all the way in. Over the course of a month I purchased fourteen succulents, all known for their hardiness and each paired with its own handmade pot selected with care on Etsy. When those didn't die, I became braver and bought two more leafy plants, a monstera plant and a money tree. I love them both dearly, but I also regret buying the money tree because I am deeply superstitious that if it dies, I will lose my life savings. My hobbies are very relaxing.

As the owner of fourteen plants—most of which survived through COVID and beyond—I am now clearly a plant mom. My chlorophyll-filled children keep me company. They surround me all day and bring light and energy into my world. Living in New York City with no personal outdoor space, I love having green so close to me. And I care deeply whether these plants live or die. I ask friends to "plant sit" when I am on long trips and keep each plant on a careful watering schedule. I don't have a 100% success rate—every once in a while, I will neglect a succulent too much while traveling or something I can't identify will go wrong. I think I've lost three or four plants since the pandemic. And they're not actual children, so I get over it. I also don't name my plants. But I do clean their leaves carefully and think about whether or not they are getting the nutrition they need and look at them lovingly and often. *(This is a section I filled in quite a bit, though it's not clear yet what needs to be kept.)*

I have saved them from being "root bound," meaning their container was getting too small, causing the roots to tangle and prevent water absorption—laying down a tarp on the floor of my Manhattan apartment for a full indoor repotting. That is the moment I knew I was a true plant mom and that I would do pretty much anything for my children. Would not recommend! But both of my children came through and they are so much healthier and happier with room to expand. *(I filled in this section quite a bit as well, as I felt it illustrated my maternal instinct and responsibilities clearly.)*

I am a person with many love languages, but tending to plants corresponds most to "acts of service." I love doing things for others to make their lives easier, even something small like swinging by the grocery store for my mom. Taking care of plants has reinforced my desire to be responsible to others, a quality that also shows in my commitment to my students, friends, and family. It has also reminded me of the rewards of learning something new and how much seeding a new interest can add to my life. Which is why, when I'm away from home and think about how my plants might be thirsty, I remember that I need them just as much as they need me. *(This was perhaps the most important section I filled in, as it explores my deepest reflections on the meaning of my plant mom role, getting to the heart of what I hope admissions will take away from the piece.)*

***

In summary, use this *snipping*, *flipping*, and *filling* process to play with your text freely. Don't be afraid to experiment with the order of your storytelling and add things you might later cut. This is the phase in which your story really starts to come alive. *(And then, if you're a good "essay mom," you learn to keep it alive!)*

WHAT IS THE STRUCTURE OF A PERSONAL ESSAY?

Many of the best personal essays tell a story. And like all good stories, they have (*drumroll*) a beginning, a middle, and an end. As you pull the elements of your freewrites into your draft, think about the order of events. Where is the turning point? Is there a lesson? What should an admissions officer know about you or the situation upfront for proper context? What should they remember about you when they finish reading your essay? Once you determine these answers, you can set up the key points by building dramatic tension. The heart of your message will often be revealed, or at least start to unveil itself, about three-quarters of the way through your essay.

Maybe breaking your leg in a pogo-sticking accident taught you a lesson about balance and prompted you to bring more literal and figurative balance to your life. Did this lead to a full recovery and your subsequent invention of pogo-stick yoga? *(Poga?)* The order in which you reveal these events does not have to be the order in which they occurred; rather, it should work to emphasize the point you find most valuable: your ability to draw inspiration from your life or your resilience in the face of broken bones.

Do you want to start your story at the chronological beginning of the action (breaking your leg)? Maybe you want to begin with the ending and flash back to the events that led up to your opening paragraph. (What does Shavasana on a pogo stick look like?) Perhaps you want to dive right into the middle of the action and unpeel the story from the inside out. (Looking longingly at your pogo stick as you're immobilized in a cast.) However you decide to organize your puzzle pieces, be sure to identify a main point and organize the rest of your story around it. *(Remember the Gargantuan Four? If not, don't worry, I'm going to remind you again shortly!)* Without a true turning point, your essay will read more like a timeline than a story. And don't look down on or outright dismiss the classic chronological layout. Some of the best college essays ever submitted have taken the form of a straightforward and insightful personal story, thoughtfully told.

OKAY GREAT, BUT HOW DO YOU START THIS THING?

I probably don't have to tell you about the importance of an opening line or paragraph—it's one of the things that's likely been drilled into you in every writing class you've ever taken. The opening is where you hook your readers. This is where you convince them it is worth their while to read more, and with full attention. And, since you know you need to grab the attention of an admissions officer who's nodding off over essays about the best summer camp experiences ever *(I fell asleep just typing that)*, you can probably guess that the opening line of your college admissions essay is especially important.

An opening line should grab the reader and pull them into a story face-first. It should surprise or intrigue. No matter how you decide to start your story, know that it needs to be compelling and signal to an admissions officer that you have come to the table with a fresh perspective or something unique and personal to communicate.

Let's examine the opening line of my "Plant Mom" essay in progress:

The only plants I owned before 2019 are now dead or were never alive to begin with.

Not a terrible attempt, but after some thought, I decided on a clearer, more active line:

I am a proud plant mom, though until a few years ago, I never met a plant I couldn't kill.

Regardless of which version I employ, my goal is to engage the reader with an opening conceit that asks more questions than it answers. What plants have I killed? What did my journey to becoming a plant mom look like? And why did I want to pursue it in the first place?

Like a piece of music whose notes can be reorganized and played in infinite sequences and styles, there are endless ways to open your story and trumpet your arrival to admissions. Here are some opening line "dos" that have the potential to sound the horn, set off fireworks, and wrap a reader up in your story:

DO

Do Open with Dialogue

Trying to envision someone's voice in your head is instantly engaging and communicates so much about the character and the writer, in just a few words.

Do Ask a Question or Set Up a Mystery

Beginning with a line that begs for an answer is a surefire way to draw your reader into your story.

Do Make Them Chuckle

Kicking your essay off with humor signals to an admissions officer right away that this just might not be another boring essay.

Do Surprise the Reader

"BAM!" A cleverly placed sound effect, a line of logic twisted on its head, or even just a description of a particularly strange detail can jolt a reader like a bucket of cold water and widen their eyes to what comes along next.

Do Break the Rules

Actually, strike that. There are no rules. Get creative. Try a thing you've never tried. Open with a sentence fragment. Get vulnerable and reveal something true about yourself. Avoid being weird for weird's sake, but free yourself to see where your imagination takes you.

Do Experiment with Endless Incarnations of Opening Lines Before Deciding Which Words Will Serve as Your Introduction to Admissions

The right opening line will make itself known, ringing clear as a bell in your head when you reread it. *(DING DING DING!)*

As you can imagine, there are also some opening line tactics that should be avoided—things that will stop admissions officers in their tracks or worse, lull them right to sleep. Here are some opening line "DON'Ts":

DON'T

Don't Restate the Question or Tell Admissions the Purpose of Your Essay

They know why you're here. Don't waste the words—just jump right in.

Don't Use a Quote from an Author or Other Famous Person

This is one of the most clichéd ways to open an essay—so clichéd it is one of the few college essay-related clichés almost always beyond saving. Unless the quote you're considering adds crucial perspective to your essay, cut it. You don't need it, and admissions officers would rather hear *your* thoughts and *your* words.

Don't Ease Us/Them In

You have 650 words, tops, to get your point across to admissions. Every word counts. Don't overexplain and don't enter your story with trepidation—dive right in and get things moving.

Don't Get Stuck on the Opening Line

Yes, a killer opening is important to your essay, but that doesn't mean you have to write it first. If inspiration fails to strike, press on. Once you've written the rest of your story and know where it's going, you'll have a better sense of how to start it.

AWESOME, BUT HOW DO YOU BUILD TO YOUR MAIN POINT?

The middle of your essay is where you want to lay out the meat of your story. It is where you will encounter characters who impact your life and where you will make choices that affect your future goals. In the outline phase of the process, you mapped out a basic order in which your events and epiphanies would unfold. As you're tinkering with these paragraphs, reorganizing your key points, and elaborating on your most important ideas, it is crucial to think about pacing. What can you do to actively pull an admissions officer through your narrative with pointed interest? Are there strategies you can use to push a story forward with a sense of urgency?

Of Course, There Are! Here are a Few of the Most Effective

1. **Keep your language active (aka use the active voice).** Another tip I'm sure you've heard in English class, maintaining an active voice throughout your essay is a reliable way to up your readers' engagement. Think about the difference between "A presentation behind the science of pizza-making was given." and "I gave a presentation about the science behind pizza-making." In the first (passive) version, you don't even know who gave the presentation! Wouldn't you rather immerse your reader in a story in which things are actually happening? Where you and your supporting characters do things instead of having things happen to them? *(Trust me, you would.)*

2. **Carefully craft your transitions.** Shoddy or abrupt transitions between paragraphs and ideas can jolt a reader out of the narrative. Unless you are employing that strategy intentionally *(which is possible!)*, take extra care to smooth out your links from one paragraph to another. Connecting your ideas in a way that feels seamless and natural keeps the reader on the ride with you, without having to pause and make the links themselves.

3. **Reveal, don't explain (aka show, don't tell).** Every personal essay is going to require some setup. How did you end up at the carnival at midnight with only one shoe? The trick is to reveal this information through engrossing details, dialogue, and other compelling language. Don't settle for a bare-bones recounting in its driest form. Give us some hearty, vibrant descriptions to latch onto. A few carefully selected details often allow you to say a lot. And in an assignment that is relegated to such a small space, it's important to be efficient with your words.

   An example from my "Plant Mom" essay:
   Before my pandemic plant adoption, I long had a sense that I wasn't a plant person. The only living things brought into my house as a child were goldfish, usually won at a carnival and "sent to the farm upstate" within days. There were no real indoor plants, just a few clusters of the fake Anthuriums that were so popular in the '80s. My mother notoriously hates cut flowers ("they just die!"), so a bouquet of fresh tulips never decorated our kitchen table.

   Through examples from my childhood, I want to show the reader why I didn't think I had a green thumb. The idea that my house growing up didn't have a single live plant *(or animal!)* in it provides insight into the elements that shaped me and my interests. *(It also allows me to try to crack a few jokes.)* The specificity of the details, like the appearance of the fake flowers or the small quote from my mom, add a ton of flavor in very few words, which is both informative and engaging.

4. **Look for confirmation.** Demonstrating a personal quality or transformation often requires more than a single anecdote. Even if your essay will focus primarily on one experience, try to demonstrate how the lessons you learned reverberated throughout the rest of your life. Including outside examples will showcase consistency and self-awareness to admissions officers. Did learning how to bake help you become more systematic about other aspects of your life? When your friend came to you for help, did you have a history of supporting each other through difficult times? Try to pinpoint moments and details from other parts of your life that will prove to your readers that you are who you say you are.

5. **Harness the power of small details.** Details make a story personal. They are what transforms an essay that could have been written by a handful of

your peers into an essay that could only have been channeled from your brain through your fingers and onto the page. Details breathe life into your story, *and* they act as the supporting evidence for bold claims. In fact, excellent details, thoughtfully integrated, can serve as both a claim and the proof at the same time.

Again, from "Plant Mom:"

> *I half-heartedly attempted to nurture multiple orchids in my twenties, ultimately neglecting them to usher in their ultimate demise. A creepy, lifelike replica of a mid-sized Audrey 2, the talking, people-eating plant from* Little Shop of Horrors, *still sits on my windowsill, the result of an Etsy commission for an obsessively authentic Halloween costume.*

Though these sentences will be further refined in future edits, I pulled them into this draft because they don't just detail my knack for starving or feeding my plants out of existence. The reader also gets a few clues about other things I'm interested in *(an obsessive commitment to costuming!)* and I reinforce my comedic voice.

SO YOU WROTE AN AWESOME STORY— ARE YOU DONE YET?!?

Not quite. The last line of the essay is just as important as the first. The opening line sets a stage of intrigue, and the closing line makes the final mark. Don't waste the chance to leave a lasting impression. The closing line can tie your story up in a neat little bow, or it can leave the admissions officer wanting more. No matter what, the final few words of an excellent essay should impart a feeling of connection with or curiosity about the applicant that the admissions officer just can't shake.

The final lines of my "Plant Mom" essay attempt to close the loop on how plants have impacted my life:

> *Tending to others and seeding new interests have become essential to my happiness. Which is why, when I'm away from home and think about how my plants might be thirsty, I remember that I need them just as much as they need me.*

These sentences summarize my main points with a sentimental bent that reflects my deep feelings for this recently acquired hobby. A little ending plant wordplay ("thirsty") also helps close the loop while emphasizing the theme.

SOME CLOSING LINE DOS

Do Tie Your Ending Back to Your Beginning

Tying up your story this way can showcase advanced writerly ability and often has a poetic effect.

Do Leave the Reader Wanting More

Leaving your readers with a final thought to ponder or an open-ended range of possible outcomes in front of them is an effective way to spark long-term ruminations on you and your essay.

Do End on Reflection

Pointing admissions officers to a lesson you've learned (without bonking them over the head with it) is often a very effective ending note that underscores the maturity you developed through your experience.

Do Try Out as Many Closing Lines as You May Need

Try new things. Edit and tweak. Keep going until your ending gives you chills.

AND, OF COURSE, SOME CLOSING LINE DON'TS

Don't End an Essay with "Thank You for Your Consideration"

I swear people do this. But your essay isn't a cover letter. Keep your reader in the moment and don't waste the last words of your essay.

Don't Leave Us Hanging

There's a difference between an intentional cliffhanger or thought-provoking teaser ending and a final line that fails to conclude the action and provide necessary closure. Make sure you're not leaving the reader in a state of confusion.

Don't Just Give Up

It's obvious when a writer grows bored of the assignment and allows themselves to mentally exit the process before that final line. I know it's challenging, but keep yourself engaged until the end. Celebratory I-finished-my-essay dance parties are soon on the way.

***

Let's assume you've written pages of freewrites, sculpted masterful opening and closing lines, and *snipped*, *flipped*, and *filled* in all the glorious points in between. You are staring at a page-and-a-half's worth of blood, sweat, and tears in the form of a personal essay but you're not sure you're 100% totally want-to-be-with-you-forever in love with what you've created. What now?

TRY A NEW LENS

The "classic memoir" is the most widely recognized approach to the personal essay: a story told directly, with well-emphasized detail and a keen eye for personal reflection. This approach can be extraordinarily effective in showcasing your passions and goals. Still, your story as told in this relatively straightforward style may not ignite the bright spark you hoped to set off for your reader. Maybe you feel like something is missing: Is there magic yet to be mined from this narrative of yours? Try filtering your essay through the lens of a metaphor or mechanism to see how your narrative takes shape.

Metaphor

A grand metaphor is just as it sounds: a metaphor so all-encompassing it frames your entire story. Filtering your story through a metaphorical comparison can unify disparate elements of your life and experiences. What are the commonalities between your various hobbies, strengths, or accomplishments? Is there a discernible theme and a creative way to describe that overlap? A secret: My "Plant Mom" essay is also a grand metaphor essay on many levels. I found personal growth through plants. I bloomed through my new hobby. I play with this language quite a bit in the essay already, but I could have emphasized it even more if I so chose. Was I a plant in need of watering before I adopted something to take care of? Do the people I care about in my life nourish and root me?

Maybe everything from the books you read to your obsession with the long-standing enigmas of science are all indicative of your love of a good mystery. A grand metaphor is also useful when you're attempting to put a new twist on a well-worn subject. For example, can you reveal the unexpected value your short stature has had on your life by discussing the impact other small things have had on you and on the world? If you decide to apply a grand metaphor to your essay, make sure your comparison holds up to a basic logic test. Do you really embody the characteristics of a tissue box? Is life really like a chocolate croissant? *(It is in my dreams.)* If your metaphor isn't excellently crafted, don't use it. And no matter what comparisons you employ, sincerity and authenticity will always be the most important elements in an essay. Regardless of how your story is structured, admissions officers should get a window into the real you.

Mechanism

If a grand metaphor isn't working for you, you can try using what I refer to as a storytelling mechanism: in essence, a hyper-stylized structural device. There is something about a good idea filtered through an interesting format that breaks the essay review monotony and demands a reader's attention. Have you thought about writing your essay as an article from a scientific journal? Or maybe an acceptance speech? Should I have written my "Plant Mom" essay as a set of instructions for keeping plants—and new interests—alive? No matter what, your mechanism needs to be well-honed to be effective. Your newspaper article should open with a lede and maintain a recognizably journalistic tone. The dialogue of your *(very)* short play should sound like believable conversation and maintain a consistent format. So what if it's gimmicky? Sometimes it also works!

Your Personal Lens

If you are staring at your essay, tearing out your hair because you don't like the look of it through any of these lenses: STOP! I like your hair. And you don't have to view your essay through a new lens to craft a good story: Remember, these filters are *tools*, not *rules*. Applicants may dismiss a memoir-style narrative because they think they have to come up with some complex comparison *(life is like a box of donuts)* or strange device *(college essay in iambic pentameter!)* to capture the attention of admissions; but remember, a straightforward narrative still leaves plenty of room for variation and creativity. Sometimes detailing the path to becoming a plant mom is enough. Some of the best admissions essays are the ones that keep things simple and true.

THE FINAL TESTS

For the first time, I am going to ask you to think about your essay's length. The word limit for the personal statement is generally around 650 words, which is the equivalent of about a page and a few lines (single-spaced), so when you have sewn together all your highlights and begin *snipping, flipping, and filling*, try to keep yourself to a page and a half or about 800–850 words. This will give you the space to create a pointed, detailed story that can be clipped down to the word limit during the final editing process.

When you have your first draft on the page, read through it. How does this story reflect on you as a person? Are there striking details to latch onto? What about descriptions and dialogue that will burn themselves into an admissions officer's brain? Does the essay hold your attention from beginning to end? Does your opener lure a reader into the action and your closer sum things up on a truly memorable note?

I also recommend you check your essay for the Gargantuan Four at this time. Remember the four elements from chapter 3 that tell you if your essay has a successful overarching theme and detailed messaging that will leave an admissions officer with a substantive, memorable impression? Can you clearly identify your topic, differentiating factor, overarching message, and admissions takeaway? If not, you likely still have some revising to do.

6 What About the Finishing Touches? Polishing to Perfection

You have reached the final stretch. Your topic has been unearthed, your heartfelt words have been mined and organized, and your story has been sculpted into a thoughtful narrative that holds a reader's attention from beginning to end. Now it's time to put in some elbow grease and Polish to Perfection. In this chapter, I'll show you how to infuse your essay with one last dash of personality, round up your remaining errors, clip out unnecessary words, and smooth out any remaining rough edges so you can present a winning piece of prose to admissions.

Of course, I'll also address your burning editing-related questions, including the following:

- What are some finishing touches I can apply to increase my essay's overall intrigue?
- How can I make cuts to achieve clarity and get my essay under the word limit?
- How can I ensure the accuracy of my facts, spelling, and grammar?
- What are some of the most common, easily identifiable errors people make on their admissions essays?
- And how do I know when I am really, truly ready for submission?

THE TRIPLE EDIT

First I'd like to note that while this step is called "Polishing to Perfection," true perfection is unachievable. *(Sue me, I love alliteration enough to employ some interpretive license.)* The editing process is meant to refine your draft, elevating it to the highest level of writing you can achieve while not driving you to incurable madness. (In chapter 9, I talk about when it's time to let go and call a piece finished, once and for all.) Polishing your draft to a high shine is accomplished through a process I like to call the Triple Edit. You will be shocked to find out that there are three steps involved here. *(Imagine that!)* They include *editing for intrigue, editing for clarity*, and *editing for accuracy*.

1. EDITING FOR INTRIGUE

The first step in the Triple Edit, *editing for intrigue*, is the act of fine-tuning the final components that will make that essay pop, sizzle, emote, sparkle, tap dance, or whatever else you want your writing to do for your reader. Here are some suggestions for how to add new features, turn up the volume, and infuse an extra layer of interest and entertainment into your final essay.

Dive into Dialogue

Dialogue can be an incredible way to showcase your own characteristics and the features of other people in your story. Take this tiny pop of dialogue uttered by my mom in the "Plant Mom" essay:

> My mother notoriously hates cut flowers ("they just die!")

I didn't have to include Mom's dialogue, but it's funny *(always a plus)*, and gives the reader a bit of insight into the household I grew up in.

Ask Questions

Ask questions of your characters in the text. Ask them of your reader. Questions can be an excellent way to reiterate a point or shift the tone of a piece in an unexpected way. It also puts the impetus on the reader to consider both your query and its potential answers. Questions are even appropriate if they're rhetorical because they help underscore your point. I didn't end up using this explicitly in my "Plant Mom" draft, but I considered including the following question in my essay:

> *Indoors, elbow-deep in soil to fix the root tangling that was preventing my plant's water absorption I thought, "Is this love?"*

Be Sincere

Don't underestimate the power of sincerity and self-awareness in essay writing. A thoroughly honest essay will always leave a deeper lasting impression than one that skims the surface and avoids hard truths. Speaking from a place of vulnerability imbues your story with conviction and heart.

> *My chlorophyll-filled children keep me company, surrounding me with light and energy. Living in Manhattan with no personal outdoor space, I love having green within arm's reach. And I care deeply whether my foliage lives or dies.*

These points make up the heart of the "Plant Mom" essay. They speak plainly about why my plants are important to me and what they bring to my life. There is power in this directness.

You should also note that healthy honesty is not the same as a confession. We all have moments we're not proud of, but your college essay is not the right place to atone for your sins, major or minor. Trust your instincts. If your story embarrasses you, save it for your diary.

Go for Those Chuckles, HAs, and LOLs

Think about it. Admissions officers run through over fifty essays a day, many of which end up being pretty serious in nature. A student who makes these hardworking people laugh is one who will be remembered. Using humor is a surefire way to telegraph loud and clear to the reader that you're a real human being, not just another academically excelling robot. It says that no matter what life throws at you, you can put things in perspective and take joy in life's absurdities.

> *I slightly regret buying the money tree because I am superstitious that if it dies, I will lose my life savings. My hobbies are very relaxing.*

Poking fun at myself for bringing anxiety into a practice that is meant to be relaxing is likely relatable in a different way and will hopefully produce some laughs as the reader thinks, "UGHHH, of course I do this."

If you're not feeling funny or you don't think humor is appropriate or cracking jokes is just not your style, don't put pressure on yourself. Laughs aren't the only way to win over an admissions officer, and being true to yourself and your voice is a far more powerful strategy than attempting to inject forced punchlines that may fall flat.

Employ a Little Wordplay

The language you choose for your admissions essay can be a compelling indicator of creativity, writing ability, and your internal thought processes. Clever descriptions, analogy, metaphor, alliteration, and other literary devices are also the phrases and comparisons that often lodge themselves in admissions officers' brains, sprouting roots and sparking remembrances when decision time is afoot. Can you find a way to describe something that an admissions officer hasn't heard before? For example, I had so much fun using plant-related words throughout this essay:

> *This is how my facility with flowers germinated and where I began to find calm in the presence of plants. Tending to others and seeding new interests have become essential to my happiness.*

Employing descriptive, analogous, and metaphorical language can add extra life to your prose and imbue your story with a unique flavor, reinforcing the theme as it unfolds.

***

If you infuse your essay with engaging dialogue, sincerity, maybe a little humor, and some crafty wordplay, you will be the anti-soporific in an admissions officer's pile of routine college admissions essays.

2. EDITING FOR CLARITY

The second step in the Triple Edit is *editing for clarity*. An admissions officer only has two to three minutes to run through your essay, so simplification is key, especially when it comes to expository passages.

Scour your essay for clunky descriptions and explanations that may not make sense to a reader encountering your story for the first time. What details can you add or tweak to get your message across?

Editing for clarity is also about cutting the excess. Up until I asked you to snip away during the story-sculpting phase of the process, my directive has been WRITE, WRITE, WRITE! NEVER STOP WRITING! MORE IS MORE. Now I'm going to stop you, hand you a pair of scissors, and give you permission to clip things out, yet again.

I know what you're thinking: "Stacey, I love my whole essay! Every line! I can't cut anything out! PLEASE DON'T MAKE ME DO IT."

I feel for you. Trimming the fat requires a certain amount of steely resolve, especially when you have been working on an essay for weeks, developing a *(plant-mom-like)* bond with every word and line. But saying less can actually have more impact. *(And don't forget those rigid word limits.)* So be merciless. If you love a sentence but it doesn't further the story, get rid of it. Here is an example from my essay:

> *My father did love to garden, and my siblings and I really liked helping him plant in the spring. We all especially loved lantanas, a flowering plant that comes in a kaleidoscopic range of color variations, many of them super pigmented (think magentas, deep oranges, vivid yellows).*

The above turned into this:

> *My father did love to garden, however, and my siblings and I helped him plant outside every spring, peppering the beds with hyper-colored lantana plants.*

Every word that appears on the page should be specific, memorable, and deliberate. While 650 words may feel like a lot when the page is blank, you may have realized that it is actually a very small space in which to tell even a modest-sized story. You also may have noticed when editing for intrigue that adding specific, colorful words can actually eliminate longer, blander phrases ("I ate all the spaghetti very fast" vs. "I inhaled the spaghetti"). You will likely need every one of the words allotted to you to get your point across, so use them creatively, economically, and with intention.

3. EDITING FOR ACCURACY

The final step in the Triple Edit is *editing for accuracy*. This is the phase of editing that includes what is known as "proofreading." Errors are your enemy, big and small. Hunt those errors down. Scare them out of their little hiding places. *(And there are sure to be a few of them hiding in plane site—I mean, plain sight.)*

Let's start by discussing the most obvious tools for wiping your essay clean of errors both careless and clandestine: your computer's spelling and grammar check and AI. Use these as preliminary guides to help identify potential errors. That said, keep in mind the many limitations of these tools. *(I know, it's sad. Sometimes technology fails us.)* Luckily for you, we live in the age of the internet, where grammar snobs and language obsessives spend their free time expounding upon the difference between "I could care less" and "I couldn't care less" for the benefit of the lost grammatical souls of the world. When in doubt, look up the rule. And, if you're still unsure, use multiple, reliable sources like Dictionary.com and the Punctuation Guide (http://www.thepunctuationguide.com/index.html) to double-check spelling and grammar rules before you implement any suggestions from the internet's more automated wordsmithing tools.

This is also a good time to do a quick fact check and make sure any claims you make or data points you reference are correct. Are you sure you were ten when the original *Jurassic Park* movie came out in theaters? *(You probably weren't born yet.)* What state is Augusta in? *(Yes, there is an Augusta in all of these places: AR, GA, IL, KS, KY, ME, MN, MI, MT, NJ, NY, SC, WV, and WI.)* It's not a bad idea to check general timelines and order of events to make sure things piece themselves together properly. And make sure any proper names and names of institutions are spelled and capitalized correctly. *(Is it the Capitol or the capital?)* Factual errors can be distracting to admissions and make you look careless and lazy. So double and triple-check your details. *(Don't think I didn't check the proper spelling of "Anthurium." I did! Twice!)*

MOST COMMON ERRORS (THAT CAN BE AVOIDED OR RECONCILED VIA A LITTLE EDITING MAGIC)

Over-vocabularizing

I know. That isn't even a word. But it sounds super fancy, so you should probably use it, right? WRONG! Un-vocabularize yourself. *(Again, I know that's not actually a word.)* Forget the thesaurus. You are smart! You don't have to be a human dictionary to impress admissions. The essay is not a test of whether you've memorized the meaning of "vociferous." *(That's what standardized testing is for!)* The essay is a test of your powers of expression. Be honest about your level of vocabulary and avoid the common pitfall of misusing a word you haven't encountered in its proper context. Besides, excessive thesaurusing can destroy directness, which we know is crucial for conveying your message in three minutes or less. Forsake splendiferousness for clarity.

Using Inappropriate Abbreviations (Aka Using Inapprop Abbrevs)

I love abbreviations and interspeak as much as anyone. *(SRLSY, I do.)* But keep them out of your final essay. Your essay should be conversational (yes, contractions are okay), but not to the point of reading like texting shorthand.

Clichés

I'm not going to *beat around the bush* here: Clichés really *get my goat*. When you take that *trip down memory lane*, telling admissions about the time you were a *mover and a shaker* putting your *nose to the grindstone*, it makes my *blood boil*. I'm a content and grammar snob, so I find clichés to be extra unappealing, but I also have enough confidence in your creativity to know that you can do better. Admissions officers know it too and expect you to *think outside the box* without using phrases like "think outside the box." So strike those tired sentences from your essay and do it now. Never put off until tomorrow what you can do today. *(It physically hurt me to utter all of those clichés.)*

BEFORE YOU HIT SUBMIT

The editing process is all about diligence and attention to detail. You've come all this way and I know your brain is tired and all you can think about is taking your bike to the beach or watching a hundred hours of YouTube. You're almost there! Still, don't send off the essay without giving it one final review. Here are a few last things to check off the list before you hit the submit button.

Take a Break Before Reviewing Your Own Work

Before you send your essay on its final journey to admissions, step away for an hour or two or even a day or two. When you get back, try reading it aloud. As much as you can, try to see your work with fresh eyes and hear it as others would hear it. Is there an awkward sentence or turn of phrase that needs some revision? Are you missing a transition between paragraphs? Do you need to briefly explain that obscure song or book you reference?

Get Another Pair of Eyes on Your Final Draft (One Pair, Not 100)

Show a parent, guardian, aunt, or uncle. Ask an English teacher you trust or an afterschool coach who cares about you. Your friends are awesome people, but they are not up to this task. Find an adult with a keen editing eye, a love of the written word, and an honest but supportive feedback style. Listen to their advice. Adjust when necessary. Reject suggestions where appropriate. Follow your gut. Other opinions are helpful for added perspective, but only you know how you want to be represented in the eyes of admissions.

Pick Your Prompt

Remember that time I told you to forget about the prompts, locking them away in a vault and acting like they never existed? I hope you remember the combination because now is the time to revisit the list. As you scan through your options, chances are one or two prompts will jump out at you as the perfect complement to your completed essay. Perhaps a prompt you didn't expect to use will shed new light on your essay, and you'll decide to make a few tweaks to fit your story to the question at hand. Whichever route you choose, all of your hard work pays off in this moment. You'll find that backing into a prompt is *waaaay* easier than parallel parking.

My "Plant Mom" essay likely qualifies for the prompt that asks students to write about an *interest or talent my application would be incomplete without*. It also represents *a time I challenged a belief or idea. (I am an irredeemable plant killer!)*

This burgeoning hobby definitely *inspired a period of personal growth and new understanding of myself*. And we know it qualifies for the *topic of my choice* prompt.

Finally, Ask Yourself a Few Test Questions

These, it turns out, are pretty similar to the ones you asked yourself in chapter 3 after choosing the topic that set you off on this essay-writing adventure. When you homed in on your ideal subject matter, you imagined everything this topic could reveal to admissions. Now you get to see if your execution has fulfilled your idea's massive potential. So ask yourself these questions:

1. Will this essay make admissions wish they could meet you in person? Does it inspire them to want to know more about you?
2. Is this essay actually about you? *(Or is it actually about your flower-hating mom?)*

3. Would anyone else be able to write this essay in the way you wrote it? Would it be crazy to think of someone else claiming your essay as their own?

4. What does this essay say about you? What is the ultimate message you are hoping to convey?

5. Do you feel good about this essay? Would you feel proud reading it aloud in front of an audience? Does it represent who you really are?

And remember that scene from admissions headquarters, where a dozen smart people sit around a table and one holds up your application and says, "Take them!" When that admissions officer summarizes you in a sentence, what will they say? *("Take the Plant Mom!" I hope!)*

Right now, my one-line synopsis of you says: You're the driven and talented student who just finished the final step in writing an effective and compelling college admissions essay. Cue the confetti! Wheelbarrow in the mountains of cupcakes! Wake up the celebratory breakdancing pandas! You have made it through the brainstorming and the freewriting. You have sculpted and polished your story until you could sculpt and polish no more. You're ready to hit the submit button, and it's time for a celebration.

But first, how about we take a peek at my fully edited final "Plant Mom" essay?

Pretend you're an admissions officer at College Essay University, and I am an applicant. As the esteemed admissions officer for the university, do you get a solid sense of who I am and what I care about from this essay? What am I trying to communicate about myself? What will I bring to your campus? *(Do you like me? Do you really like me?)*

ADVICE IN ACTION: PLANT MOM ESSAY— THE FINAL DRAFT

I am a proud plant mom, though until a few years ago, I never met a plant I couldn't kill. This includes the orchids I half-heartedly attempted to nurture and a cactus I watered into oblivion in my twenties. In fact, the only plant I managed to keep alive was never alive to begin with: a creepy replica of the people-eating plant from *Little Shop of Horrors* that still sits on my windowsill, the result of an Etsy commission for an over-the-top Halloween costume. My knack for helping real plants thrive didn't emerge until I was stuck inside during the pandemic. My first leafy purchase in social isolation was a snake plant, which the internet said would be virtually impossible to kill. The care instructions were easy enough to follow: Water, put on a sunny windowsill, ignore, repeat.

Before my pandemic plant adoption, I assumed I wasn't a plant person. The only living things brought into my house as a child were goldfish, usually won at a carnival and "sent to the farm upstate" within days. My family owned no real indoor plants, just a few clusters of the fake Anthuriums popular in the '80s. My mother famously hates cut flowers ("they just die!"), so fresh tulips never decorated our kitchen table. My father did love to garden, however, and my siblings and I helped him plant outside every spring, sprinkling the beds with hyper-colored lantana plants. As a young adult, I discovered I loved having flowers in my home (sorry, Mom) and started taking lessons on Japanese flower arranging, known as ikebana. This is how my facility with flowers germinated and where I began to find calm in the presence of plants.

During the first year of COVID, flowers were hard to come by, and I missed my ikebana practice. A snake plant had to do. Much to my surprise, I kept my new botanical acquisition alive, its sturdy green leaves reaching skyward. I have always been a collector, and once I become fixated on something, I go all the way in. So, over the course of a month, I purchased fourteen succulents, all known for their hardiness and each paired with its own carefully selected pot. When those didn't die, I became braver and bought two more leafy plants, a monstera and a money tree. I slightly regret buying the money tree because I am superstitious that if it dies, I will lose my life savings. (My hobbies are very relaxing.)

Now, as the owner of twenty-five plants—most of which survived COVID and beyond—I am definitively a plant mom. My chlorophyll-filled children keep me company, surrounding me with light and energy. Living in Manhattan with no personal outdoor space, I love having green within arm's reach. And I care deeply whether my foliage lives or dies: I ask friends to "plant sit" when I travel and maintain a careful watering schedule. I even repotted my largest plants on a tarp in my apartment last year to save them from being root-bound. Indoors, elbow-deep in soil to fix the root tangling that was preventing my plants' water absorption, I thought, "This is love."

I am a person with many love languages, but tending to plants corresponds most to "acts of service." I love doing things for others to make their lives easier, even something small like swinging by the grocery store for my mom. Taking care of plants has reinforced this desire, a quality that also manifests in my commitment to my students, friends, and family. It has further reminded me of how exploring a new hobby can add to my life. Tending to others and seeding new interests have become essential to my happiness. Which is why, when I'm away from home and worry that my plants might be thirsty, I remember that I need them just as much as they need me.

***

Because I am not immune to the need to test my own work as I suggest you do yours, let's take a look at what I identified as my Gargantuan Four:

Topic: How I became a plant mom who loves taking care of things/people.

Differentiating Factor: Memorable, easily recallable focus on plants; intriguing opener that contrasts being a current plant mom with being a former plant killer; plant-related language play peppered throughout; instantly brandable as "the Plant Mom essay."

Overarching Message: My exploration of a new hobby during COVID revealed my desire to tend to others and seed new interests, qualities that are valuable in many areas of my life.

Admissions Takeaway: I am someone who loves trying new things, isn't afraid to get my hands dirty (literally and figuratively), and loves doing things for others.

***

And there you have it. If I can do this, I know you can, too. Okay, now you can cue the confetti. And though you may have run through all the major steps of effective essay-writing with me, I'm not finished dishing out advice. Continue on for guides to tackling the school-specific supplements, debunking of the most common college application essay misconceptions, and sage advice on maintaining a positive mindset throughout the essay-writing process. Sometimes it takes more than seven hundred cookie breaks to keep an essay writer motivated *(not that I would know from personal experience)*, and I have some techniques that will help you push through even the toughest college essay roadblocks.

7 What Are Those OTHER Admissions Essays? A Quickie Guide to Supplemental Essays, the UC Personal Insight Questions, and More

You've just put the finishing touches on your personal statement. You've got a hundred Spotify playlists and YouTube videos lined up and you're just about to swear off writing another application essay ever again when you find them: the school-specific supplemental assignments.

What are these other essays the University of Michigan says you have to complete? How many questions is Columbia asking you to respond to? What is this evil folly?

These are the school-specific supplemental essays, a curse placed on both the houses of students and admissions officers alike.

If the personal statement is the Loch Ness monster of college essays *(massive, lurking, initially scary but ultimately conquerable with the power of your mind)*, the supplemental essays are the gremlins *(there are a lot of them, they can be annoying, and you definitely shouldn't feed them after midnight)*. The good news is that the strategies you have honed in earlier chapters are directly applicable to these assignments. The bad news is that there are often a lot of supplements to complete—an increasing number every year. In this chapter I'll clarify the purpose and strategy behind writing a few of the most pervasive types of supplemental essays. I'll also answer questions like these:

- What is a supplemental essay and why does it matter?
- What are the most common supplemental essay topics and how do you answer them?
- What do you do if admissions throws you an oddball question?
- Are there secrets to crafting a good short-answer response?
- What is the additional information section?

- How can you organize your school-specific supplemental essay prompts for maximum efficiency?
- Where do you even find these magic prompts?
- What if a school you are applying to uses its own independent application instead of a platform like the Common Application?

Let's address your first question about supplemental essays and why they matter, which likely takes the form of "WHYYYY?? WHY ARE THEY DOING THIS TO MEEEEEE?"

Contrary to popular opinion, admissions committees all over the country aren't sitting around long conference tables, laughing evil laughs as they conjure up additional ways to torture you and devour all your spare time. Believe it or not, these supplemental essays serve a purpose.

WHAT IS A SUPPLEMENTAL ESSAY AND WHY DOES IT MATTER?

As the overall undergraduate applicant pool grows, as it has just about every year for the past two decades, colleges have struggled to find reliable ways to distinguish the students who are passionately committed to their institutions from the ones who are on the fence or "just applying because my guidance counselor told me to." Most supplemental essay assignments are designed to both gauge a student's interest in the school at hand and determine where a student might fit into a school's community. Typically, these essays focus more on future academic and professional goals, school-related activities, and your role in your current community than they do on self-reflection and creativity *(though incorporating those elements is always encouraged)*. Unlike with the personal statement, the specifics of the supplemental prompts matter very much, as there are small variations in queries and instructions that must be followed for each school. Still, while the number and complexity of these essays does seem to grow each year, there are a few usual suspects that regularly appear in the lineup. Let's start by discussing those garden-variety hobgoblins and how to approach them.

THE WHY ESSAY

The "Why Essay" is one of the most plentiful little monsters popping up to spook you during the application process. It also happens to be one of the most fruitful in enabling an admissions officer to understand a student's motivations for applying to their college, providing applicants an opportunity to consider what their life and education at a particular college will entail. The *why* essay essentially boils down to this: Why do you want to go to the school in question and what will you do when you get there?

This shape-shifting question comes in many forms, some long, others comically short; some focus solely on academic objectives, while others are expansive enough to include reflections on the school's culture and vibe. It attempts to solicit information like: "How will you take advantage of all the resources a school has to offer? How will a school support your academic or professional goals? And how do your past experiences or future goals support your objectives?"

Why essays can quickly veer into incredibly generic territory. Specifics are necessary in crafting a personal and engaging read, as are two essential components of a successful *why* essay: in-depth knowledge of a school and a convincing demonstration of personal interest.

Both of these elements require you to actually know what any given institution has to offer. And how do you find that information out? Research! The good news about doing research in the internet age is that you don't have to visit a school to become intimately familiar with its campus, curriculum, and culture. Whether you're tasked with writing a *why* essay for a school or not, it's never a bad idea to spend a few hours immersed in a target school's website, trying to get a feel for the culture and combing for reasons you might be interested in attending. This process, of course, is extra important if the school you're exploring *does* assign a *why* essay. Showcasing your knowledge of and interest in a school's offerings in detail separates the truly impassioned from the perfunctory applicants. As you page through the website, poke around your departments of interest. Is there something specific in the curriculum that calls out to you? A professor's name that you recognize? Are you excited about the school's green-living-focused volunteer community? Maybe you want to join the school's nationally recognized a cappella group or participate in the freshman class's 100-year-old tradition of putting on footie pajamas and studying outside in the snow during the week before finals. *(To my knowledge this is not an actual tradition at any university, but that doesn't mean you can't make it one!)*

For those of you lucky enough to visit the schools to which you are applying in advance of writing your essays—take full advantage. Hop on a campus tour and ask your guide about their experiences. *(Do not ask them where the best parties are. Don't worry—you'll find them.)* Take down your tour guide's name and ask for an email address so you can follow up with questions. Make friends with someone in the cafeteria. Notice how the campus makes you feel and try to reflect on why you are feeling those feelings. Was there an air of collaboration on the main quad? Maybe an exciting lab you discovered or a mock newsroom you would love to have access to?

After you complete your visit or research session (and I mean *right* after), take a few minutes to jot down notes on everything so you remember the important details when you sit down to write a month after your visit. You might even want to devote a formal freewrite to each school. When you wrote your personal statement, I asked you to get specific about yourself—now is the time to get personal about your interest in your education and life at each particular school. What special programs within your major address your interest in the overlap of business and technology? Is there a lab mentorship opportunity in which you're eager to participate? Make sure your essay is specific to each particular college; if you can insert the name of any other school into your essay ("The professors are top-notch and I am excited to study with my fellow students on the quad"), return to your notes or the school's website and find more original, more personalized information to convey your goals and interest.

Also, I know I shouldn't have to say this, but don't plagiarize. If you find a class that interests you, talk about it in your own words; avoid using a word-for-word class description in your essay. Give admissions a little *(or a lot of)* credit. They know what their websites and catalogs sound like.

Once you have a solid map of your school-specific interests, it's time to turn the lens back on your experiences. It's one thing to say you want to join the elite marine biology program, but it's much more convincing if you also mention that you spent a summer on Cape Cod studying the migration patterns of humpback whales or that you write a blog about your favorite deep sea "current" events. *(See what I did there?)* Don't expect admissions to make the connection between your transcript, activity list, and your interest in their school—build the bridge for them.

Since all schools word their *why* essay prompt slightly differently with varied requests and word counts, it's critical to read each prompt closely, follow instructions carefully, and answer each question in its entirety. *(Please note that these prompts can change from year to year, and you should confirm the exact wording and qualifications of each school's prompt for your current application cycle.)* Here are some examples:

From the **University of Michigan:**

Describe the unique qualities that attract you to the specific undergraduate college or school (including preferred admission and dual degree programs) to which you are applying at the University of Michigan. How would that curriculum support your interests? (Required for freshman applicants. 550 words maximum.)

This is a fairly straightforward, academics-focused *why* essay. The 550-word maximum gives applicants a lot of space (almost as much as the personal statement!) to detail their interests and objectives as they showcase their familiarity with the University of Michigan's offerings. Extensive research into the degree and curriculum of interest is required, as is building links between your academic interests and your past pursuits. All in all, this is a classic academic *why* essay prompt.

The **University of Wisconsin–Madison** takes a slightly different approach to the long-form *why* essay, asking a more open-ended question that allows space for reflection on the school's culture and community before it requests applicants zero in on academic objectives.

> *Tell us why you would like to apply to the University of Wisconsin–Madison. In addition, please include why you are interested in studying the major(s) you have selected. If you selected undecided, please describe your areas of possible academic interest. (You may enter up to 650 words, but 300–500 is recommended.)*

Rice splits the question into two prompts, first asking separately about a student's academic goals before opening up the field. Notice that both prompts are quite a bit shorter than the examples above, forcing students to be especially judicious with their words.

> **1.** *Please explain why you wish to study in the academic areas you selected. 150-word limit.*
>
> **2.** *Based upon your exploration of Rice University, what elements of the Rice experience appeal to you? 150-word limit.*

As the word limits get shorter, you will be challenged to select just a few of the most important and personal connections you have to a school and its offerings. For example,

> *What is your sense of **Duke** as a university and a community, and why do you consider it a good match for you? If there's something in particular about our offerings that attracts you, feel free to share that as well. (250-word limit)*

> *Please tell us why you want to attend **UMass Amherst**. (100 words or less)*

One hundred words or fewer? **UMass** has to be joking, right? *(I wish.)* Here, you will learn to be economical with your words and precise about your passions and qualifications. Choose one or two elements of a school's program or environment that appeal to you for highly specific reasons and expand on them. When you inevitably spill over the word limit, take out your pruning shears and cut any last word that isn't essential. You'll be amazed at how much you can fit in a small space when you're intentional in this way.

PRO TIP: It is easy to get mired in the details of your research for these questions, but don't forget to channel your unique voice. A clever opening and closing and some vivid language throughout can go a long way (if you have the space, of course), especially in a sea of "I want to go to the University of Michigan because..." default introductions.

In summary, when it comes to the *why* essay *(as with so many admissions essays)* details are important. What piques your particular interest in your dream school? Your *why* essay, whether it's 100 words or 600 words, should clearly demonstrate the connection between the school's characteristics and your own unique personal qualities and experiences. In the biz, we call that your "fit."

THE ACTIVITY ESSAY

The "Activity Essay" is another common supplemental essay troll, but as with all of these pesky school-specific assignments, it's quite useful in revealing compelling information about yourself to admissions. While admissions will ask for a list of your activities as part of the main application submission, the descriptions on the activity list are often limited to ridiculously low character limits. *(Not word limits—character limits! They're very, very short.)* This means your space to convey the motivations behind your most important endeavors is limited. But admissions is still interested in hearing your deeper reflections about these pursuits, hence the *activity essay*. How has your commitment to an activity had an impact on your life? How has participation in this activity affected the lives of others? Maybe your membership in speech and debate served as the inspiration for your future pursuit of a law degree. Did your afterschool volunteer work at an animal shelter bring new furry family members into the lives of your friends and family? Has playing the guitar since you were five years old shown you the power of dedication and allowed you the thrill of taking part in your own garage band?

One of the keys to a successful activity essay is to expand on, not repeat, what you write in your activity section. Admissions will already know if you've won awards or placed nationally in FBLA competitions. How did participating in FBLA spark a love of entrepreneurship that led to your creation of a small tech venture? This is an excellent place to highlight your leadership skills, teamwork, and drive, but remember: Show, don't tell (if you have the space). Describing how your role as captain improved communication among your cheerleading teammates is much more effective than telling admissions, "I'm a great leader."

Below are some examples of how the activity essay might show up on your applications, starting with the **University of Florida**:

Please provide more details on your most meaningful commitment outside of the classroom while in high school and explain why it was meaningful. This could be related to an extracurricular activity, work, volunteering, an academic activity, family responsibility, or any other non-classroom activity. (250 words)

"Meaningful" can be interpreted in many ways: Maybe you work in a soup kitchen every Saturday and struck up a deep friendship with one of your fellow volunteers that changed your perspective on segregation in your city. Perhaps joining the theater club at your high school and learning how to deliver a monologue helped you conquer your lifelong stutter. Your story doesn't need to be dramatic or life-changing to be meaningful: You could write about your weekly Sunday dinners and the gradual shift in your perspective and responsibilities as your grandma's health declined and hosting duties moved from her house to yours. Whatever you choose to write about, make sure that it reveals something about your character, perspective, and interests.

I personally love that the **University of Florida** suggests that what you cover in this prompt can include employment experience, family responsibilities, and more *(all of which can be activities that shape you in a meaningful way)*. **Harvard**'s prompt is similarly broad:

Briefly describe any of your extracurricular activities, employment experience, travel, or family responsibilities that have shaped who you are.

Did working at Cold Stone Creamery help you come out of your *(candy-coated)* shell as you mixed candy-coated chocolate into your patrons' ice cream? Remember, any topic is fair game as long as you thoughtfully and accurately respond to the prompt. Just try to avoid writing about the same thing in two different essays; I've said it before and I'll say it again: Your essays are your only chance to address admissions directly, so make sure that you share as much as you can about the multi-faceted person you are.

As with the *why* essay, the *activity* essay may seem straightforward, but don't forget to channel your authentic voice and writing style as you describe your ascendancy to debate master or adventures teaching chess to middle schoolers. The more your energy and enthusiasm for these activities shows in the writing, the more compelling they—and you—will be to admissions.

THE COMMUNITY ESSAY

The "Community Essay" prompt hopes to solicit insight into how you operate in a community and what you might contribute to your new college environment.

It mines for information about your social habits, favorite causes, and shared passions. Where do you feel like you belong? What can you expand on *(that hasn't already been covered elsewhere)* to show your versatility, passion, and ability to connect with the world around you?

The word "community" might sound straightforward at first, but it's a term that leaves itself wide open to interpretation. Community might refer to your family history, heritage, or background. Were you raised in a Senegalese community in Harlem and are you excited to celebrate your heritage and customs by joining or creating a Senegalese club on campus? *(Don't forget to research to see whether the school in question already has one!)*

Community might be a group that is defined by club membership or commitment to an organization. Maybe you belong to a nonprofit whose mission is to provide water safety classes to children and young adults in your lakeside hometown. Did you inspire a group of teens to get their lifeguard certifications in an effort to keep the lake area safe during the summer months?

I also love when students address what I call "theoretical communities." These are collections of people with shared interests that might not be officially defined, but that absolutely exist and impact their members' lives. Are you part of a community of sports fans around the world who can connect with other strangers over the amazing play in a recent game? Are you obsessed with the weather and connected to a forum of other "weather heads" *(Is this a thing? It's probably a thing.)* who follow storms and exchange predictions? *(Will it rain in NYC tomorrow? Asking for a friend.)*

Theoretical communities allow students to highlight information about themselves beyond school activities and background information that might be covered in other areas of the application. And it can be fun for admissions to see you use creativity in the way you interpret these questions.

So what counts as a community? The answer is almost anything.

Your Community Could Include—But Is in No Way Limited to—the Following

- Geographic communities (your city, state, or country)
- School communities (STEM, student council, choir, sports team)
- Online communities (fantasy football, book club, subreddit)
- Interest-based communities (K-pop fandom, LARPing, improv)
- Identity-based communities (race, ethnicity, gender, sexuality)

If you feel like a contributing member of a collective unit, you're operating within a community that can—in one way or another—be defined. Don't overthink it! Instead, focus on what that community adds to your life and vice versa. I advise applicants to write authentically about their experiences while reflecting on the impact of their background.

Of course, the way colleges pose their community essay prompts can vary. This community essay prompt from **Northwestern** has a future-oriented bent:

> *Community and belonging matter at Northwestern. Tell us about one or more communities, networks, or student groups you see yourself connecting with on campus. (200 words)*

What kind of community member do you hope to be on a college's campus? What do you hope to share with others about your lived experience? How will you incorporate this element of your identity into your life at school? It never hurts any applicant to spend a little time on your top college's website to find out more about the place you hope to call home for the next four years. If you can connect your community experiences to the college's mission, culture, and/or values, all the better. These kinds of prompts offer applicants the opportunity to paint a picture of how they'll leave their mark on campus, while providing insight into what they've accomplished and invested themselves in thus far.

Tufts provides a little extra direction, reminding you to include "a specific example or two." *(Which is a good idea even if a prompt isn't directly asking for it!)*

> *Using a specific example or two, tell us about a way that you contributed to building a collaborative and/or inclusive community. (200–250 words)*

Washington University's community prompt reminds applicants that it's critical to highlight their role within the community they choose.

> *WashU supports engagement in the St. Louis community by considering the university as "in St. Louis, for St. Louis." What is a community you are a part of and your place or impact within it? (250 words)*

This question doesn't just ask you to define your community—it wants you to explain the impact you've made on the people, issues, and environments you've cared about.

As with all of your application essays, remember to be as authentic and as specific as possible when addressing community essay prompts. Those tiny details that may seem insignificant can really bring a story to life and pull a reader in. It's also in your best interest to reflect on and articulate what your community has meant to you. Has it made you feel like you have a place in the world? That you belong somewhere? Has it introduced you to new people, ideas, and languages? Has it impacted the way you interact with and understand the world as you know it?

THE DIVERSITY ESSAY

The "Diversity Essay" provides students a place to describe their background, culture, and values. It often gives admissions important context for a student's résumé, transcript, and other application materials. And, it can offer a crucial opportunity for students of color to discuss their experiences in white-dominated spaces.

It's worth celebrating the preponderance of opportunities to address race, gender, and other identity-oriented qualities on college applications. Universities want to enroll a cohort with varied backgrounds, experiences, and belief systems; encouraging a wide range of perspectives is what makes these institutions such havens for deep inquiry, spirited debate, and enlightened progress. Throughout history, privilege has begotten privilege *(and, let's be real, it still does)*, but a conscious attempt to combat bias and value the perspectives that have been historically devalued can only enrich education and society as a whole.

So please, if you're a student of color and you feel so inspired, use this essay to describe your efforts to elevate the work of underappreciated Black women writers at your school. Or discuss why it's so important to you to insist on the correct pronunciation of your Indian name.

That said, just because you come from a nonwhite heritage or underrepresented background doesn't mean you have to write about it here. The beauty of the college application is that *you* get to decide how you want others to see you. You can define yourself based on what you, the applicant, think is important. So follow your gut.

If you don't have an obvious response to a diversity prompt, don't worry: Admissions is not trying to stump you. They understand that their applicant pool includes many students who do not come from what are considered traditionally diverse backgrounds, which is why these prompts are often crafted with room for interpretation.

Consider this prompt from the **University of Virginia**:

> *What about your individual background, perspective, or experience will serve as a source of strength for you or those around you at UVA? Feel free to write about any past experience or part of your background that has shaped your perspective and will be a source of strength, including but not limited to those related to your community, upbringing, educational environment, race, gender, or other aspects of your background that are important to you. (250 words)*

Prompts like this can seem daunting to unpack at first, so I always recommend that students break down their options. For UVA, a student can write about their background, perspective, *or* experience. The background, perspective, or experience you choose can be related to any one of the following: community, upbringing, educational environment, race, gender, or other aspects of your background. *(It doesn't get more open-ended than that, folks!)* Finally, admissions wants you to showcase how your topic has served and will continue to serve as a source of strength in the future.

Here are a few examples of potential subjects that combine these options and don't hinge on race, gender, or what students might describe as obvious components of "diversity" (though those can certainly be elements in these essays, if applicable):

- Perspective + upbringing + strength = a student who grew up with a single mom writes about how they matured early under the influence of a strong female role model. This has fostered independence, resourcefulness, and respect for others.
- Experience + background + strength = a student works as a host at a restaurant, encountering a wide range of patrons and team members, improving their communication skills, and internalizing the values of hard work and collaboration.
- Perspective + community + strength = connecting with an online community of Magic: The Gathering players allows a student to embrace their authentic interests and emboldens them to launch an in-person club at their school, ultimately finding kindred spirits while developing leadership and interpersonal skills.

Let's discuss another prompt, this time from **Swarthmore**:

Our identities and perspectives are supported and developed by our immediate contexts and lived experiences—in our neighborhoods, families, classrooms, communities of faith, and more. What aspects of your self-identity or personal background are most significant to you? Reflecting on the elements of your home, school, or other communities that have shaped your life, explain how you have grown in your ability to navigate differences when engaging with others, or demonstrated your ability to collaborate in communities other than your own. (250 words)

This prompt asks students to identify aspects of their self-identity or personal background, but again, these can be interpreted widely. Maybe a student is a natural teacher, and their patience has enabled them to make meaningful connections with students in the special-education program where they volunteer. Perhaps the host from the restaurant in the UVA answer above learned about world cuisine during staff meals before their shift, exchanging recipes and stories with the cooks about favorite dishes made by their grandfathers. Has your experience in the drama club required you to inhabit someone else's circumstances in a way that activated empathy and inspired you to action? Has injustice in the world sparked you to join a protest, watch the news with your parents every night, or build a coalition in your community? This question shifts some of the focus from your origins and identity to how that background informs your behavior, which presents a great opportunity to talk about the ways in which encounters from your everyday life inspire you to be more considerate of and engaged with others.

This does bring me to my next tip: Avoid exaggeration. As with pretty much every application essay, the key to a successful response is authenticity. I hope I don't have to remind people to be honest, but I'll just say it: Don't lie about your background. It's wrong, and if admissions finds out you're not really 15 percent Native American, there will be consequences (and rightfully so). Also, don't try to make meaning where there is none. Your dad might be Irish, but if that background hasn't infiltrated your own life or impacted you in a meaningful way, that might not be fodder for a resonant essay.

Finally, be extremely careful about how you frame your experiences with other cultures, especially if you are coming from a place of privilege. Avoid saviorism. Ask yourself this question: Am I making myself the hero of this story when I shouldn't be? You may have participated in a school walk-out related to the murder of George Floyd, but *why* did you do it? What did you learn? What did you not know that maybe you wish you had known earlier? Humility is powerful when writing about interactions with the culture of others, and the desire to absorb and really listen is key. If you're presenting yourself as an ally, be a true ally. Recognize the ways in which privilege has protected you and acknowledge that; as much as you have learned, there is always more to know.

THE ODDBALL ESSAY

The *why, activity, community,* and *diversity* essays are all fairly common, and topics for these essays are likely to be a bit more obvious to you than the subject of the personal statement. But what do you do if one of the schools you're applying to throws you an oddball?

There are schools, like the University of Chicago, that have historically taken pride in developing quirky questions for their applicants to answer. In recent years, more schools are jumping on the bandwagon, luring students to their applications with questions like: *You've invented a time machine! When and where is your first destination and why? (150–300 words)* (**Scripps College**). This is both fun and exhausting for applicants who are grateful for an injection of modern, quirky inspiration, but whose creative wells are running dry. *(You know I love these oddballs because I'm an oddball—and an essay nerd.)*

Let's look at a couple of these wacky questions together. Consider one of the past prompts from **UChicago**:

Orange is the new black, fifty's the new thirty, comedy is the new rock 'n' roll, ____ is the new ____. What's in, what's out, and why is it being replaced? (One- or two-page response. About 500 to 600 words.)

Breathe. You know how to do this. Consider what they're asking and dig back into your repertoire of subjects you haven't yet discussed. Maybe you think strawberry jam is the new guacamole because you've recently gotten into canning. Perhaps you believe ultimate Frisbee is the new football. Culling your own interests and passions will help a lot here.

Let's look at an **Emory** prompt:

Which book, character, song, monologue, or other creative work (fiction or nonfiction) seems made for you? Why? (100 words)

Emory's looking for more than a book report or the lyrics to your favorite song. Instead, focus on what this piece of art means to you. How does it connect with your personality, values, circumstances, or future goals? Did you relate to Devi's immigrant family on the show *Never Have I Ever*? Do you play Sia's "Unstoppable" as a pump-up before every volleyball game because the lyrics make you feel powerful?

Pomona offers an even more opaque prompt:

At Pomona, we celebrate and identify with the number 47. Share with us one of your quirky personal, family, or community traditions and why you hold on to it. (150 words)

Perhaps you and your dad used to drive through your neighborhood to find shortcuts through the cul-de-sacs, and you've continued doing this with your younger brother now that it's your job to teach him to drive. Maybe your blended family created new rituals when you all moved in together, like starting each week with a family huddle where everyone shares what they're most looking forward to that week. Maybe you and your baking-obsessed friends have a rotating "bake-off" each month where you try to replicate the challenges from an episode of *The Great British Bake-Off*.

If answers don't come to you immediately, don't panic. There are two tricks to these essays: First, start early. *(Duh.)* Brainstorming time is key for cracking the code to these puzzles. Read through the wild prompts that have been slung at you and remember what you learned in chapter 3: Go outside. Live your life. Think things through. The ideas will come.

The second trick: Work backwards. I will talk more about essay organization later in this chapter, but subjects for other supplemental essays often end up fitting into the oddball framework when filtered through a quirky lens. For example, take another past UChicago prompt: "Create your own spell, charm, jinx, or other means for magical mayhem." When looking through your other supplemental essays, maybe you find one you wrote about being trilingual and your spell—which allows people of all backgrounds and languages to communicate—uses a hybrid of the three languages you grew up with. Chances are, if you've written about a topic for another, more straightforward supplement, it is important enough to convey to admissions once you adjust it to fit a less-expected perspective.

SHORT ANSWERS

There's. One. More. Popular. Format. For. Supplemental. Essay. Questions. It's the short answers. *(Your responses to which can be funny, unlike the dad joke I just tried to pull.)* These little critters provide a different kind of creative challenge for aspiring college-goers. Take this set of short answer questions from a prior **Yale** application:

> *Applicants submitting the Coalition Application or Common Application will also respond to the following short answer questions, in no more than 200 characters (approximately thirty-five words):*
>
> *What inspires you?*
>
> *If you could teach any college course, write a book, or create an original piece of art of any kind, what would it be?*
>
> *Other than a family member, who is someone who has had a significant influence on you? What has been the impact of their influence?*
>
> *What is something about you that is not included anywhere else in your application?*

Two hundred characters is not a lot, which means the challenge of answering these questions lies half in generating honest, unique, and clever ideas, and half in being concise. Humorous answers can also have heavy impact here. My advice to you: over-brainstorm and overwrite. Think of as many ideas as you possibly can for each short answer and get them all on the page. When narrowing down your choices, think about representing a range of your personality traits and interests. If you say the overlap of food and science inspires you intellectually in response to the first Yale question above, don't say you will teach a class on molecular gastronomy in response to the second *(though I would absolutely take that class)*—use that space to elaborate on something totally new that admissions officers might enjoy knowing, like your encyclopedic knowledge of classic French films. Once your general plan for your answers is solidified, you can cut and condense your way under the limit.

A few more examples for you to ponder, first from the **University of Maryland**:

To tell us more about yourself, please complete the following prompts using only the space provided (650 characters).
If I could travel anywhere, I would go to... *
The most interesting fact I ever learned from research was... *
In addition to my major, my academic interests include... *
My favorite thing about last Friday was... *
Something you might not know about me is... *

While you must follow the format of completing the sentence fragments with these, still use as much creativity and variety as you can in your answers. Would you travel to Tokyo for cherry blossom season to feed your flower and sushi obsessions? *(I can vouch for that experience and those interests!)* Did you learn *(and were you appalled by)* the meager number of women who make it to top-level positions in Fortune 500 corporations, inspiring you to start a nonprofit for lifting up young female entrepreneurs? Was your favorite thing about last Friday that you stayed up late to finish your annual re-read of *The Lord of the Rings*? How can you show, in a relatively small space, the range of your interests and pursuits?

How about one more set for the road *(because I love these)*, this time from **USC**:

Describe yourself in three words (25 characters each).

The following prompts have a 100-character limit:
What is your favorite snack?
Best movie of all time:
Dream job:
If your life had a theme song, what would it be?
Dream trip:
What TV show will you binge-watch next?
Which well-known person or fictional character would be your ideal roommate?
Favorite book:
If you could teach a class on any topic, what would it be?

These USC prompts are meant to be short and direct. *(25 characters! Eek!)* There's still room to represent your diverse passions, but succinct answers will have to do a lot of heavy lifting here. Admissions is truly just trying to get a sense of what you like, though you can sneak in some information about yourself through your voice.

Is your dream trip to the elven settlement of Rivendell? Would your ideal roommate be Wylie Dufresne, king of modern molecular gastronomy? *(Also, see how we can repurpose answers from one set of short answers to another here? Fun, right?)*

A Note on Optionality

Some of the school-specific supplements will be listed as "optional" components of their related applications. This means that, for example, you can submit your Duke application without penning a response to any two of the optional prompts. But why would you? Each additional essay written provides another opportunity for you to spotlight your values, beliefs, and motivations for admissions, speaking to them with authenticity and conviction. And think about it: If you're an admissions officer, don't you want to admit the student who has put in the effort *(and it is a lot of effort!)* to think through and construct thoughtful responses to all questions posed? As a result, I consider most "optional" essays to be, for all intents and purposes, not optional.

There will, however, be the occasional instance in which an optional question truly does not apply to you. If an optional prompt asks you to discuss your gender identity and you either don't have anything substantive to say or don't want to share this information with admissions, by all means, skip it. I would never encourage you to generate false perspectives to fill space or write about something you might not feel compelled to share. But if you have additional opportunities to differentiate yourself from other applicants and you do have something interesting to say, by all means, say it!

ADDITIONAL INFO ESSAY

Many application platforms (including the Common App) offer an optional "Additional Information" section. While most school-specific optional essays are not truly optional, the essays in *Additional Information* really are. On the Common Application, the Additional Information section consists of two parts: the Challenges and Circumstances prompt and a space for—you guessed it— additional information. As always, it's critical to check the current application for exact wording and length limitations, but here is an example of what you are likely to see in this area of the application:

Challenges and Circumstances

Sometimes a student's application and achievements may be impacted by challenges or other circumstances. This could involve the following:

- *Access to a safe and quiet study space*
- *Access to reliable technology and internet*
- *Community disruption (violence, protests, teacher strikes, etc.)*
- *Discrimination*
- *Family disruptions (divorce, incarceration, job loss, health, loss of a family member, addiction, etc.)*
- *Family or other obligations (care-taking, financial support, etc.)*
- *Housing instability, displacement, or homelessness*
- *Military deployment or activation*
- *Natural disasters*
- *Physical health and mental well-being*
- *War, conflict, or other hardships*

If you're comfortable sharing, this information can help colleges better understand the context of your application. Colleges may use this information to provide you and your fellow students with support and resources.

Please describe the challenges or circumstances and how they have impacted you. (250 words)

The breadth of subjects that can be covered in this essay is wide, but all fall in the category of extenuating circumstances or life-altering experiences that likely impacted your academic career and extracurricular opportunities. The goal of this essay is to directly and succinctly contextualize the challenge(s) at hand, providing admissions with a clear understanding of your circumstances. Did an illness during your sophomore year cause an overall drop in your GPA? Do you have a learning difference that wasn't diagnosed until your freshman year? Did taking care of your sick grandmother prevent you from playing varsity tennis after being a star on the team for two years? Did a natural disaster leave you unhoused for part of your sophomore year, preventing you from focusing on your studies?

You may not want to focus on a hardship in your personal statement—especially if you don't believe these circumstances define you and/or don't want them to be the main focus of your written application. Still, life can be unpredictable, and you have every right to want to explain to admissions how life has laid down hurdles on the road to your goals. So use this space to fill that gap and save the personal statement for painting a bright picture of the things that make you *you*.

A note of warning: Most students who write a challenges and circumstances essay will be writing about undeniable life challenges. Your problem with procrastination or disappointment with your standardized test scores should not be featured here. Consider what other applicants might be writing about and be thoughtful in your assessment of your own struggles, large and small.

Additional Information

This is the more nebulous of the two optional Common App Additional Info section prompts. Any major hardships you've faced should be covered in the challenges and circumstances essay above. While it is tempting to use this space to explore another random subject of your choosing, students should use it sparingly. Admissions is already wiped by the time they get to this section and trust me, if they wanted to read another essay from you, they would have asked for it! With that in mind, let's examine what this prompt might look like.

> *Please provide an answer below if you wish to provide details of circumstances or qualifications not reflected in the application. You may enter up to 300 words.*

In other words, unless you have something crucial to add or explain—and there is absolutely nowhere else on the application for you to write about it (including the challenges and circumstances essay)—you should probably leave this space alone. Rare exceptions include the potential addition of a research abstract or short description of a substantive project that isn't featured elsewhere. But really and truly, do not feel pressure to fill this space. The unrequested, extra information you stuff in there is unlikely to hurt you, but it also probably won't help.

ORGANIZING SUPPLEMENTS FOR MAXIMUM EFFICIENCY

Let's do a quick pulse check. Is your heart racing? Is your head spinning? Are you already drowning in an ocean of your own sweat just thinking about all these supplements? Don't worry. I swear, it's really not that bad.

I'm here to introduce you to your friend, overlap.

I started this chapter discussing some of the more common themes and subjects explored in supplements. Even outside of the *why* essay, *activity* essay, *community* essay, and *diversity* essay, you are going to discover there is much repetition among your supplemental essay prompts. To tackle these essays as efficiently and effectively as possible, I suggest that before you brainstorm a single word for these assignments, you collect every single supplement required of you and organize them.

For example, it's likely you will have to write *why* essays for multiple schools. Which one is the longest? Start there. As long as the programs you're applying to are similar at each school in question, some detailed research and fact-swapping will allow you to use your initial skeleton as a base for future essays of the same ilk. And as we discovered with the personal statement, it's often much easier to cut an essay down than it is to add to it. You don't have to reinvent the wheel. Important note: If you're using the same essay as a base for various supplements, make sure you check and change your facts and references carefully. There is nothing like a beautifully written essay that ends with "and that is why I belong at Vassar" to get the Bates admissions officer shaking her head and tossing you into the rejection pile.

Once you finish attacking your *why* essays, round up your *activity* essays and again, tackle the longest one first. By the time you make your way to your *community* essays, *oddballs*, and other miscellaneous assignments, you will have a stack of ideas to comb through *(since you never throw anything out)* and a ton of drafts to mine for fully polished content. Subjects from finished essays may even be usable if you simply look at them through a different lens. Maybe apply a metaphor or a mechanism? The trick is staying organized and approaching these essays without fear.

WHAT IF A SCHOOL I'M APPLYING TO ISN'T ON THE COMMON APPLICATION OR A SIMILAR PLATFORM?

Many schools will allow you to submit via a platform like the Common Application or Coalition Application. These platforms collect your personal details, activity descriptions, personal statement, and other main application components to ship off to the schools of your choice, along with each one's supplemental assignments. The idea is that you don't have to reenter your basic information every time you send out an application. *(So convenient!)* But there are still a few schools that encourage or require submission through their independent platforms.

In the past, Georgetown has required a personal statement that is similar to the Common Application's statement along with a few supplements. For application platforms that mimic this setup, aside from entering your information into a new platform, your strategy for working on the essays will mirror that of your other schools: personal statement first (likely copied word-for-word from your Common App version), and then the school-specific supplements.

The MIT and UC applications are different, however; neither requires a long personal statement. Instead, students are asked to submit a set of short essays. These are some of the **MIT** questions, though again, the essays change from year to year so please check the current year's prompts and use these only as an example:

Depending on the question, we're looking for responses of approximately 100–200 words each. There is also one final, open-ended, additional-information text box where you can tell us anything else you think we really ought to know:

What field of study appeals to you the most right now? (Note: Applicants select from a drop-down list.) Tell us more about why this field of study at MIT appeals to you.

We know you lead a busy life, full of activities, many of which are required of you. Tell us about something you do simply for the pleasure of it.

While some reach their goals following well-trodden paths, others blaze their own trails achieving the unexpected. In what ways have you done something different from what was expected in your educational journey?

MIT brings people with diverse backgrounds together to collaborate, from tackling the world's biggest challenges to lending a helping hand. Describe one way you have collaborated with others to learn from them, with them, or contribute to your community together.

How did you manage a situation or challenge that you didn't expect? What did you learn from it?

You'll notice many familiar themes here, including a *diversity* essay prompt, an *activity* essay prompt, and an academic *why* essay. What's extra notable is that you will have your personal statement at your disposal for answering these prompts, as well. Even if MIT is your tippy-top choice, my recommendation is this: Write the personal statement first. It will always be useful to you in these rogue non–Common App situations, and it is helpful to have the Loch Ness monster off your plate before you start tackling these shorter answers. Additionally, writing the personal statement will help you define some of the most important points you want to make about yourself to every admissions committee—which you will then want to incorporate into at least one of your MIT short answers.

I suggest you approach the **University of California** prompts in much the same way: Instead of a personal statement and multiple supplements, the UC application asks students to respond to four out of eight of what they call "Personal Insight Questions." What follows is just an example of what might be in store for you—check this year's prompts carefully.

Choose 4 of 8. (350 words each)

1. *Describe an example of your leadership experience in which you have positively influenced others, helped resolve disputes, or contributed to group efforts over time.*

2. *Every person has a creative side, and it can be expressed in many ways: problem solving, original and innovative thinking, and artistically, to name a few. Describe how you express your creative side.*

3. *What would you say is your greatest talent or skill? How have you developed and demonstrated that talent over time?*

4. *Describe how you have taken advantage of a significant educational opportunity or worked to overcome an educational barrier you have faced.*

5. *Describe the most significant challenge you have faced and the steps you have taken to overcome this challenge. How has this challenge affected your academic achievement?*

6. *Think about an academic subject that inspires you. Describe how you have furthered this interest inside and/or outside of the classroom.*

7. *What have you done to make your school or your community a better place?*

8. *Beyond what has already been shared in your application, what do you believe makes you a strong candidate for admission to the University of California?*

Again, you're bound to see some familiar themes in these questions. The prompt about your greatest talent or skill aligns closely with the personal statement prompt about your background, skills, and talents. Writing about an academic subject that inspires you could very well lead to a discussion of your major and what you hope to study. And "what have you done to make your community a better place?" We've seen that one before.

Even if you are hoping to attend a school within the UC system, if you have at least one school that requires a longer personal statement, complete that essay first. I guarantee you will be able to cut a gleaming chunk out to use for one of the personal insight questions. And the other UC prompts are bound to have some overlap with other supplements, as well.

For the record, it is not that I don't value the MIT and UC applications enough—especially if they're part of your first-choice submission—to give them full attention before the schools that require longer personal statements. I just value efficiency *(i.e., your time)* more! And, after many years of working with students on these assignments using a range of orders and techniques, I've found that getting the personal statement under your belt first relieves pressure and sets the rest of your applications up for success, whether they require that assignment for submission or not.

**

Is that enough? Should we talk about more essays? That pretty much covers what's required, but I can invent some if you like?

Just kidding, we're all tired. By the time all the supplements are squared away each year I, like you, never want to see another college admissions essay in my life. *(Then I regroup and start to miss them!)* But before you retire from this pursuit indefinitely *(and me for a few months)*, let's do some final checks to make sure the essays you've crafted are completely sound before you send your glorious application package off to admissions, shall we?

8 What If You're Doing It Wrong? Myths, Misconceptions, and Mistakes

You probably never thought this day would come, but here you are. Over the last seven chapters, you have learned why the college admissions essay matters and what the personal statement prompts are really asking. You have blazed your way through Backwards Brainstorming, Freewriting Your Face Off, Sculpting Your Story, and Polishing to Perfection. You have mastered how to take down any prompt from the personal statement's Loch Ness monsters to the supplemental gremlins. You have eaten roughly one thousand celebratory cookies.

You came. You saw. You conquered. You are an essay master.

Still, I know how easy it is to second-guess yourself in a process this complex and weighty. The only thing more prevalent than college applicants in an admission season are the myths and misconceptions about what the college admissions essay "should be." You're not allowed to write about community service. Don't talk about politics. You can't reference summer camp. Don't write about hardship. You *must* write about hardship. Don't express potentially controversial views. Don't use contractions. And on and on.

This chapter will dispel the rumors and illuminate the refreshing truths. It will offer a buffet of "dos" and "don'ts" and prove to you how open the topic field truly is—if you use your common sense and think creatively.

In this chapter, I'll also answer the following questions and more:

- Which topics are off-limits? *(Spoiler alert: None of them are.)*
- Does your essay have to be weird to make an impression?
- How important is using high-level vocabulary—especially if your vocabulary isn't high-level?
- Do you need to write about overcoming a challenge?
- How important is authenticity versus trying to cater to admissions' perceived wants?

Let's dive in.

COLLEGE ESSAY DON'TS

Don't Rule Out Ideas Before You Fully Explore Them

Whether you realize it or not, you are a well of rich ideas just waiting to be tapped. You're a treasure chest of golden nuggets begging to be discovered. You are a field of fragrant flowers just yearning to be…You get the point. You have a lot of great ideas—you just need to give yourself time to get them all out of your brain and onto the page where you can assess them, tune them, trade them, move them around, add to them, and admire them. This goes for brainstorming, freewriting, and even story sculpting and editing. Give yourself enough time to consider everything on the page before you toss anything. Maybe a topic you came up with isn't perfect but it has the potential to bloom when combined with another half-baked concept. And no topic is off-limits until it has been fully explored. You'd be surprised how small, strategic adjustments can turn a topic that feels like it's on the edge of viable into a brilliant vehicle for displaying your strengths and talents. Keep all of the pieces in play until you are positive you no longer need them.

Don't Try Too Hard to Come Up with Ideas That Are Quirky, Versus Authentic

So your life isn't like a bowl of all-organic quinoa. Big deal—you couldn't figure out how to arrange your story about your science fair volcano accident into a series of meaningful haiku. *(Science fair mountain. Vinegar, baking soda. The kitchen's a mess!)* Admissions officers only value quirk in an essay if it serves a purpose. In fact, they would prefer to get to know the real you: the you who cares about animals and art and found a way to combine those interests in a clear and concise piece of writing. You don't have to be weird and neither does your essay; you just have to be you. On a related note…

Don't Forget That the Essay Is About YOU and No One Else

It makes sense that, when presented with the challenge of writing an essay about your intangible qualities, you would feel compelled to focus on a person who has influenced your life outlook and philosophy. Maybe your grandmother taught you how to live in the moment as an eighty-year-old who still drives and does the tango at her geriatric singles club. Perhaps your father's love of mathematics inspired him to get you involved in robotics projects when you were a kid, which later evolved into one of your greatest passions. Writing about people who have had a great impact on your life is absolutely fair game—just make sure the main emphasis of the essay is not on the life of your mother or brother or piano teacher, but on the relationship and its effect on you. You can write your (awesome) grandmother's biography in your college creative writing class. *(I would love to read that.)*

Don't Repeat Your Résumé

Admissions officers already have plenty of lists to read. They're scanning your transcript, reviewing your activity résumé, and assessing your family background and history. I have mentioned this many times, but it bears repeating: The essay needs to reveal something that cannot be gleaned from your transcript or test scores. It is the only chance you will have to speak to admissions directly and in your own voice, so it should push beyond highlighting your academic strengths and afterschool activities and dig into the meat of who you are as a human. If you are a varsity soccer player who spends most of your time kicking balls down the field, the instinct to talk about all of your athletic accomplishments is totally natural—but try to push beyond the basic recap. Why are you such a successful soccer player? What does your ability to make a winning play on a sprained ankle say about your level of determination? Where else does this resolve show itself in your life? Reach to define those intangible qualities that make you an interesting person—someone an admissions officer would want to have a conversation with—and let the test scores and résumés speak for themselves.

Don't Tell Admissions What You Want Them to Know: Show Them

Are you fun and creative? Are you resilient and kind? Do you have passion for the things you do? The best way to communicate these kinds of qualities is to craft stories that illustrate these points. If you think you're resourceful, maybe you should write about that time you turned a spilled paint accident into an abstract set design for your last school play. What does this story say about your positive attitude and creativity? Leading a reader through events that communicate something about your inner qualities is much more convincing than a mere declaration of your purported strengths. So, don't brag; let your story do the talking instead and know that describing events and bringing an admissions officer along for one of your proudest moments is much more powerful than blatant self-congratulation. All of that being said…

Don't Sell Yourself Short

You might be one of those people who looks around at their peers and thinks, "I don't do any of the cool stuff they do." ("I'm boring!") But remember, you are *not* boring. You're a unique human with a potpourri of fascinating attributes. *(You are also probably humble and have a natural gift for identifying and celebrating the talents of others.)* So what if you haven't been to Spain to experience true Catalan culture and put your language skills to good use? Who cares if you can't dance on the wing of a plane while founding fifteen charities and curing all of the world's ills? Sometimes life's biggest lessons are found in the smallest moments and most humble achievements. Don't put yourself down or hide your talents under a pile of doubt, comparisons, and dirty socks. Give yourself some credit—I know you deserve it. Also know that life experiences, regardless of what they are, are not what make a college essay successful: It's the voice and heart of the writer that add the true magic.

Don't Be Negative

It's true in life and in admissions: No one likes a party pooper. Whether you are talking about a moment of failure or a moment of triumph, a funny story or a sad one, positivity is an essential component of the college essay. As I know you have seen in your academic and extracurricular endeavors, attitude is everything. It is what drives success and, just as importantly, it's what makes people want to be around you. If a situation is laden with heavy consequences, try to access the bright side of the story as well. Stay upbeat and deliver an epic dose of "can-do." Make sure your essay leaves the reader with a feeling that you are the kind of person who would make any day brighter, not darker, and who always looks for the good over the bad.

Don't Add Extra Words Just to Increase the Word Count

Most personal statement instructions suggest you submit an essay of 500–650 words; and while you will have to get your story under the word count maximum, you shouldn't feel pressured to hit that upper limit (certainly not on the nose). In fact, 600 words can be more than enough to tell your story if you follow our earlier tips on being economical with your language. Worry about telling your story first. If your word count is clocking in at more than 50–100 words below your allotted word count, that is when you might want to think about what in your story still remains unsaid. But with a limit of 650, a story of 599 words is likely doing the job just fine. So is a story of 610 words. Or 649. If you feel you have told your tale well, no matter what the final length, you can wear your unique word count as a badge of pride.

Don't Skip the Final Edit

So, you went on a month-long archaeological dig to excavate memories and milestones for your brainstorms, hunkered down in a subterranean lair to freewrite for seventy-two straight hours, and performed painstaking surgery to pluck the best pieces from those freewrites and arrange them with care. You're done, right? WRONG! There is no substitute for good old-fashioned editing once you have a near-final draft in place. Walk away from your essay for a day or two and come back to it with a fresh pair of eyes. *(Maybe wearing heart-shaped glasses?)* Comb through the essay slowly and methodically, looking for those errors your eye learns to skip over. Also, having a trusted advisor scour your essay for final errors is always a good idea. Someone who hasn't memorized your essay *(like you probably have)* will catch the extra spaces, missing articles, and *(GASP!)* overused exclamation points that you don't. Is there anything worse than reading your essay just after you've pressed the submit button and realizing a double "and" has made it into your masterpiece? *(No, there isn't.)* Don't take any chances. Uncover those last pesky typos. Polish that essay to a high shine.

Don't Plaigarize and Use AI Responsibly

I don't think I have to say this to you, but I'm going to say it anyway: Don't copy other people's work. It's dishonest and unethical. Also, it sells you and your talents short. We know you are an interesting and talented person who can write your own college admissions essay. And admissions officers want to read what you have to say. I hope this isn't the case, but if you're even tempted to copy someone else's work, know this: Admissions officers can sense when your work is not your own. In fact, I even suggest you take care to comb for small, unintentional acts of plagiarism before submitting your final draft. Are you sure you attributed all your information correctly? If you think you might have copied even just a factoid from Wikipedia verbatim, change it.

And be very careful if experimenting with AI tools. Perhaps surprisingly, I am not a blanket rejector of generative AI. I know students are using it and that resistance is futile; but I also believe it has a host of brilliant applications. AI can be helpful at different stages of the writing process, particularly for students who feel stuck during brainstorming. That said, admissions *will* know if a digital engine is penning your essay without significant intervention from your beautiful human brain. I can tell within seconds if an essay is predominantly AI-authored. Both for the sake of your college essay and the boatload of written assignments that are in your near future, learn to be a responsible user of generative AI tools. Know that the information compiled from random corners of the internet by imperfect technology is not reliable and that every fact and detail requires further confirmation via the application of your own critical thinking skills. Trust that your own creativity, logic, and humanity are far superior to those of a language learning model, no matter how advanced. *(My human brain and heart know this for sure.)* Don't give admissions a reason to doubt your ethical compass. When in doubt, defer to your own words and thoughts and believe in yourself over the bots. *(Though let's not make them mad in case they take over. Hi, friendly robots!)*

* * *

Those are a bunch of things you shouldn't do. And now for all the fun things you are going to want to do! Do all of these all day long every day! 'Til the cows come home! 'Til the sun goes down!

DO

Do Start Early

The most valuable asset an applicant has in the college essay-writing process is time *(along with the belief that everyone has a story to tell, of course)*. Rome wasn't built in a day, and most great college essays are not pulled together in one fretful night. *(Or week, even!)* Starting early provides the time needed to sift through topic ideas, export massive amounts of freewriting onto the page, organize and structure your story, and polish, polish, polish! An essay that has time to simmer and cook for a while—one that you can taste and adjust and sample again until you know you have it just right—is going to be much more successful than its ready-in-two-minutes microwaveable counterpart. Plus, the process of cooking up a winning college essay is much less stressful *(dare I even say, fun?)* when you have time on your side.

Do Organize Your Work

I have a secret for you. I often leave dishes in the sink for more than twenty-four hours. My bedroom is reprehensibly messy. I cannot keep track of my iPhone apps for the life of me, and I only know where my shoes are because they are laced to my feet. However, when it comes to college essay files, I am hyper, almost criminally, organized and you should be, too. It is important to label your drafts as you work in a way that is systematic and searchable. I recommend labeling files with your essay name and date. This kind of organization will help you enormously as you move forward. Knowing approximately when you created each version is critical when you're scouring for a detail you've left in a past version.

Do Be Authentic

Nothing is less convincing to an admissions officer than a story that feels fabricated or lacks heart. A school is interested in who you are, what you value, and what you will add to their community. You don't need to fake it. Be real. Work with everything you've got. *(And you've got a lot!)* Sincerity and truth are going to be some of your most effective personal sales tools.

Do Brand Yourself

I don't just want you to be yourself, I want you to be a deliberate version of yourself. A systematically selected, distilled embodiment of the most amazing YOU you can be. What are you trying to communicate about yourself to admissions? Are you generous? Are you motivated? What is that phrase your admissions officer will attach to you after reading your essay? *(Plant mom alert!)* Are you the Graduation Speaker? Are you the Donut-Eating Runner? Make sure you can boil your message down to a simple, concrete description. That will ensure you leave a deep impression in an admissions officer's mind.

Do Take Calculated Risks

The word "calculated" is important here. You need to be able to separate a good risk from a bad one. Telling a story about that time you got caught stealing a carton of ice cream from CVS? Probably not a good risk. *(Stealing is bad, even if ice cream is involved.)* Writing about the time you challenged your school's administration in defense of a friend? That sounds like it could be a story worth sharing. When it comes to risk-taking in your essay, don't ignore your instincts. Is one of your references too saucy to submit to the admissions board at Yale? If you have to ask, you probably already know. I want you to be creative and dabble outside of your comfort zone—especially during brainstorming and freewriting—but don't unnecessarily push your luck or you'll end up in the rejection pile.

Do Choose Your Advisors Wisely

College essay writing can be a daunting process, and you are likely going to want to get some advice along the way. That said, there are a few things to consider when choosing whom to entrust with your words and your *(potentially fragile)* essay-writing ego. Consult with people whose advice you trust, but whom you also know will give you nonjudgmental, constructive feedback. Additionally, stick to one or two opinions—tops. We know it's tempting to send your near-final draft to your

English teacher and your best friend, and your best friend's Aunt Trudy, who once judged a writing competition in 1972, but spare yourself the agony of sifting through a million varied opinions. What makes for a successful essay is ultimately subjective, and if you ask a hundred people what they think of your writing, you are bound to solicit conflicting opinions. Stick with the clear, refreshing advice of one or two people rather than muddying up the waters.

Do Listen to Your Gut

You have so many valuable things to say, and ultimately you are the one who knows best how you want to say them. Trust what feels right. Reject what feels wrong. When you read through your final essay, does it sound and feel like you? Are you happy with the messages you're communicating? Regardless of what even your most trusted mentor or advisor says, *you* are the only one who knows the answers to these questions. Trust yourself. When it comes to the subject of you, guess what? You're the expert.

Do Entertain

Think about what might make admissions officers smile. Maybe they will be sucked into the momentum of your fast-paced story or drawn deep into the emotional core of your hyper-personal revelation. Maybe they will simply chuckle aloud at your description of your skateboarding aunt or smile as they think about that time they took a similar kayaking trip down the river with their father. You want a total stranger to come to your essay knowing nothing about you, and leave feeling better acquainted with the person you are and curious about the person you're going to become—and you want them to feel like the two or three minutes spent reading your essay was time well spent.

Do Submit to the Relatively Random Nature of the Process

At the end of the day, when all the essays are written and all the submission buttons pressed with the shaky force of your nervous fingers, all that counts is that you have done your best. A huge hunk of the admissions process is determined by a combination of luck and a host of other circumstances that are out of your control. Maybe the school is looking for a tuba player, and you just don't play the tuba. So try to relax. Craft the best package you can, send your applications off to land on your target schools' internet doorsteps, and be proud of yourself. You have written multiple thoughtful, well-constructed college admissions essays.

You have explored the frontiers of self-reflection and searched even the dustiest corners of your brain for crafty ideas, new twists on well-worn subjects, unexpected wordplay, and disarming honesty to reel in your admissions officer and win their loyalty and affection. Now all you can do is cross your fingers and your toes, pray to the ice cream gods, and take what happens in stride.

Do Call for Help

If, after reading this page, you're wondering if your topic is worth its weight in cookies; if you're considering whether your story structure is strong enough to support your big idea; even if you're just wondering whether or not your overall story will create enough fireworks to hold the attention of an admissions officer for your allotted two minutes of admissions essay fame, seek professional help. My trusty team and I are hanging in our offices in New York City, waiting to dispense more sage advice via our one-on-one advising services. So visit our website (collegeessayadvisors.com), email us (info@collegeessayadvisors.com), call us 347-927-9CEA(9232)—send a singing telegram or a smoke signal if you have to. We will personally help extract winning ideas from your noggin with our magic powers *(of conversation)*.

Don't forget that you can always reread or consult key chapters of this book for a refresher on the college essay's purpose, process, or mindset. I know you can do this. *You* know you can do this. You have so many stories worth telling. Now you just have to seize the opportunity, open your computer, and begin your journey to college essay success.

9 Am I Going to Lose My Mind? Staying Sane During a Stressful Process

All right, applicant. You have a job to do and you know how to do it. That was the hard part, right? Or is the hard part getting yourself in the chair to get this party started? Maybe it's sustaining the energy and creativity to Backwards Brainstorm and Freewrite and Sculpt and Polish while also blocking out the noise of a process that is often fraught with pressure and high self-expectation?

There are probably a few students out there who are immune to the stresses and blockages inherent in the application process, but those people are in the minority *(and may very well be modern evolutionary miracles)*. The rest of us face all the normal fears and hurdles that come along with having ambitious goals and aspirations for our futures. So if you've wrapped your brain around the mechanics of personal essay writing but still feel intimidated by the process, you're not alone. The college essay jitters have varied causes and can manifest themselves in several different ways—and I'm here to help you squash those stresses and crash through those ugly impediments. In this chapter I will show you how to manage your mindset during the essay-writing process so you can perform at your very best. And of course, I'll answer all of your writer's block and stress management-related questions, including these:

- Why, oh why, do you have writer's block?
- How can you get rid of it?
- What are some preventive measures you can take to combat this condition?
- And what do you do if you're a chronic procrastinator?
- How can you maintain a positive mindset throughout the essay-writing process?
- What if you want your essay to be *perfect*?
- When you think you're done, how do you let your essay go?

Let's start by discussing every student's worst nightmare: I know you know that feeling. Your mind is fuzzy. You're not really feeling like yourself. Every time you sit down in front of the computer your head hurts and your fingers cramp. You try to hold onto your thoughts, and they just fly away into the ether, never to be salvaged again. You've come down with an icky, sticky case of writer's block, a condition that, when it has its grip on you, feels like it will never, ever let go. And this kind of virus is the last thing you need on your journey to college essay completion. The usual tonics and treatments are not good enough; this is an ailment that needs a specialist's attention.

Luckily for you, I earned my degree in Anti-Frustrationism, finished my rounds at Stuck-in-the-Mud Hospital, and am officially certified to treat even the most aggravated case of Advanced Writer's Block. In fact, I have pioneered the science of Writer's Unblockology, experimenting with hundreds of students—and myself—to find the cure for this incredibly pervasive affliction.

There are a variety of causes for writer's block, but among the most common are the following:

COMMON CAUSES OF WRITER'S BLOCK

Fear of Failure

Nothing gets an otherwise competent writer to clam up like the worry that whatever they make will not be good enough. This often launches students into the throes of what I like to call the "procrastination doom loop," an endless cycle in which you convince yourself that the terror and unease you feel about writing your essay will be mitigated or even subside completely if you push the task off until tomorrow. Of course, when tomorrow arrives your fear is only heightened because you have even less time than you had yesterday to Read and Then Forget the Prompts; Drill Around and Drill Down; Snip, Flip, and Fill; and Triple Edit. Of course, lack of time = more stress.

Not Having Enough to Do or Having Too Much to Do

Most likely you will be working on your college essays over the summer or at the beginning of your senior year of high school and both scenarios can breed college-essay-related lethargy. Why sit down to freewrite when you can float on a unicorn-shaped pool toy in the sun? Who has time to find a topic when there's also a pile of math assignments and a history project to complete? Still, sticking with the essay-writing process throughout both the busy and slow times in your schedule keeps your creative muscles warm and makes you less likely to run into a disheartening block along the way.

Constant Distraction

How are you supposed to put together a coherent thought, let alone a cohesive story, if you're constantly checking your social media feeds for pictures from that karaoke party? Wait, who's texting you now? And did your BFF just send you a video of a bunny that was adopted by a deer in the wild? Socialization is important *(especially when it involves cute animal pics)*, and social media is an ingrained part of our lives and culture. Still, when it's time to get serious about writing your college essay, silence the noise and give yourself some room to develop ideas without the constant tug of alerts and notifications.

TIPS FOR KICKING WRITER'S BLOCK

Regardless of the origins of your writer's block, the treatment for this ailment can come in many forms.

Lower Your Standards

Not like, forever. Just for the beginning of the process. You will raise your expectations of yourself later as you *snip* and *flip* and refine and polish. When you start, quality is not the issue; the issue is that you turn that scary blank page into one filled with ideas *(even ones that you think are silly and/or useless)*. Garbage writing days happen to the best of us *(to me more than I'd like to admit!)*, and just because you don't love the words you put down yesterday doesn't mean you've lost the magic or that you won't find that spark again today.

Silence Your Inner Critic

On a related note, I forbid you from labeling your ideas as garbage. In fact, you shouldn't be assessing the value of your ideas at all, especially if you're on the verge of feeling stuck. Shut down that critical voice in your head. Negativity does not breed creativity. I've said it before and I'll say it again: Don't think. Just write. Ideas you don't like today might shine bright in the light of a different mood on a different day.

Set Up Opportunities for Small Victories

So you can't polish off your entire essay today. Can you write a paragraph? How about one line? Take small steps. Chip away at the wall piece by piece. Remind yourself of how you dug in a little bit more yesterday than you did the day before. Every inch you type gets you closer to the final draft.

Change the Scenery

In chapter 4, I talked about setting yourself up for writing success by choosing your ideal writing location. Sometimes you might feel like working from the comfort of your own room, while other days you might benefit from the hum of a coffee shop. When you're feeling uninspired, switch it up. Take your laptop to the park or do the work in your Uncle Bob's barber shop if that feels right in the moment. *(Also, get a trim?)* A change of scenery introduces new stimuli, exposing you to different sights, sounds, and even smells that have the potential to shift your mood and knock new ideas loose.

Take a Break

Set your alarm and make sure you stand up once an hour to stretch your legs. Take your dog for a walk. Go to the kitchen and make yourself the perfect peanut butter-and-jelly sandwich. *(Proper ratio for peanut butter vs. jelly = 2 to 1. You're welcome.)* Do not just sit at your computer feeling frustrated and allowing yourself to sink into a pool of despair. Get moving. Kick a ball. Knit those next few rows of your scarf-in-progress. Carve out space for the things that brighten up your world, put you in a good mood, and make you feel like the most positive and competent version of yourself. And carry that happy energy back to your draft.

Also note that there is a fine line between not feeling like doing something *(see "procrastination doom loop")* and giving your writing or brainstorming session a real try before deciding you need to walk away. If you feel like you've hit a wall or like the Force just isn't with you, don't push it. Give yourself some space to clear your head so you can come back to your work fresher and with a little more Jedi writing power.

Start Over

It's not a fun thing to think about, but it happens. You spend hours slaving over your carefully planned essay, sculpting each word and carving away at every paragraph but no matter what you add, no matter which sentences you flip, you just aren't picking up what your essay is throwing down. You have tried every solution you can think of. *(Really.)* You have stepped away from the essay, come back to it, and still hated it as much as a snail hates salt. You know in the core of your soul that this piece of writing is not emitting the sparkle you know is necessary to distinguish yourself from the crowd.

It's time to bring up a clean document *(without throwing out the old one, OBVS)* and start a global revision. Maybe it's time to think about your topic from a new perspective? Will a slightly altered timeline simplify and embolden your text? Can a grand metaphor make connections that weren't solidifying in your earlier draft? Try to think of one big cog in the wheel to move around or replace—and then give things another shot. As always, you can consult your freewrites but give yourself a chance to get some new thoughts down on the page, as well.

PREVENTING WRITER'S BLOCK

When it comes to conditions like writer's block, I'm also a big believer in preventive medicine. There are a few things you can do to preempt that giant wall from sprouting up in front of you.

Write Every Day

Start as soon as your junior year ends and the summer begins. Write *(or audio journal and transcribe)* for at least fifteen minutes a day; that's all you need. You can describe ordinary events or reflect upon random topics as you feel inspired. Like why you like strawberries but not strawberry-flavored things. *(It me.)* Or how some words are completely untranslatable into another language and whether these linguistic differences affect people's perception of the world. The point is to keep your brain warm and ready for that essay-writing action when you decide the time is right to scan those personal statement questions *(before forgetting about them)* and dig into the process of Brainstorming Backwards.

Digital Detox

I already mentioned the potentially harmful effects of social media on your essay-writing focus, but believe it or not, the constant stimulation can actually cloud your brain. *(It's science!)* Shut down your devices for an hour or two each day. Give your brain a rest and set aside some time to power down and *get bored.* Your brain will rebel against this state of general ennui and generate random thoughts and memories on its own if you create the space.

Start Early

I've said it so many times I'm borderline nagging you, but if at all possible, you want to start this process early. Feeling a little stuck on July 15 (with a November 1 deadline) is far less likely to throw you into a tailspin of panic and clog up the works than having a bad writing day on October 15. A fluffy cushion of time will usually ease the pain of the process and ensure your heart rate remains normal.

HELP, I'M A CHRONIC PROCRASTINATOR!

But what if it's too late to plan in advance? What if you're speed-reading this book a week before the deadline? Do you feel the weight of a Mack truck on your shoulders? Are you worried that you can't do this? As a reformed procrastinator myself, I'm here to tell you that you can. *(And that you're not alone.)* Is this the ideal situation? Maybe not. Can you still slay the college essay dragon with some intensive training, a lot of concentration, and some good old-fashioned positive thinking? You bet. A few helpful suggestions as you dig in:

Don't Beat Yourself Up

This is probably not the first time you've left something to the last minute, and it may not be the last. Your tendency to put things off or leave things until the last minute doesn't make you a bad person or mean that you don't care. I still love you. *(It's true.)* Make the best of the time you have and don't waste energy being upset about things you can't change.

Cancel Your Plans

Did you think you were meeting up with your best friend to get ice cream later? I'm super sad to inform you that no, you're not! For once, ice cream can wait. Don't make your situation worse by procrastinating more. I still believe wholeheartedly in the importance of taking breaks—but ultimately your process must be more about work than about rest, especially when you're down to the wire.

Focus on the Positives

Mainly, that it's all going to be over soon. In fact, procrastination is often used as a coping mechanism by perfectionists who care *too* much about the results of their endeavors, leaving them with only a small amount of time to obsess over the final product. See, you just wanted your essay to be perfect! *(More on that later.)* Whatever the case, time is going to pass quickly and you're almost out of the weeds.

***

Now, am I suggesting that you leave your essay until the last minute? No way. And a tendency to procrastinate is curable if you find the right incentives. At the very least, demise via procrastination can be limited if you simply take some time *(in advance!)* to wrap your head around how long it will take for you to complete each element of the college essay-writing process.

Regardless of whether you decide to get down to business in the summer or the fall, three months in advance or three days in advance *(though seriously, are you trying to give yourself—and your parents—a heart attack?)*, I have some helpful tips to share for maintaining your sanity during the essay-writing process.

HOW TO TAKE CARE OF YOURSELF AND MAINTAIN YOUR SANITY

These tips may seem basic, but in the midst of college essay madness they can be easy to forget.

Hydrate

Don't underestimate the importance of H_2O. Lack of proper hydration is often cited as the cause of mid-day fatigue and can lead to a decrease in alertness and concentration—which sound like things you might really need to write a masterful college essay.

Eat

Hanger is real. Ask my close friends and relatives and they will tell you that you don't want to be around me when my tank is running low. Whether you get a crippling case of the cranks or simply do a little late-afternoon fade when your lunch wears off, make sure to keep snacks handy to feed your brain and keep you energized. Foods containing good fats like avocado and coconut pack a real high-energy punch, while protein-rich nuts are good for brain function and are highly snackable. Forget the Sour Patch Kids *(I know, I love them, too)*, which could cause you to crash mere minutes after zinging your energy into the stratosphere. Eating healthy foods instead of snacks crammed with sugar will ensure your energy lasts longer and that your body is nourished in the process.

Cry

Holding in your emotions is exhausting. If you feel like shedding some tears, I'm here to hand you the tissues. *(Not physically, but know that I'm emotionally supporting you.)* Open the ducts and let out some salty water. Then blow your nose, wash your face, do something fun to pick up your mood *(hug a puppy?)*, and try again.

Move

Get a little old school. Go outside and feel the wind on your face while you stretch your legs. Or maybe you like doing push-ups in between paragraphs. Perhaps a dose of afternoon yoga will help stretch both your muscles and the borders of your creative mind. *(Remember poga from chapter 5?)* Exerting this kind of energy is a clear stress reliever. Exercise also provides what I like to call "accidental idea time." When you go for a run or a swim or a bike ride, your objective should be to think about nothing. A mind that is allowed to fully unwind is a mind whose best ideas are free to float to the surface.

***

What if you have identified the cause of your writer's block and tried out these tips for wiping it out of your system, but you are still feeling stressed? If eating handfuls of peanuts, taking Miffy for a walk, and sweating it out haven't helped you clear the hurdles in your way, don't freak out: The stress you're feeling is totally normal, and you could benefit from a slightly more experimental stress-reducing strategy.

TWO-MINUTE CURES FOR THE HOPELESSLY STRESSED/BLOCKED

I have long been a skeptic when it comes to activities that require me to talk to myself—or that prevent me from talking to anyone else. But science actually backs up the power of some of the following exercises. Though they may seem a little woo-woo at first, the truth is that when you're desperate for relief from college-essay anxiety, you may be willing to try something a little out there, especially if it has the potential to soothe your fried nerves. So if you find yourself hyperventilating over your opening line or simply want to recharge before you dive into your fourth *why* essay, give these exercises a try. You may be pleasantly surprised at the power a posture, a few words, or some silence can have on your mentality.

Strike a Power Pose

According to Harvard social psychologist and famous TED Talker Amy Cuddy, the way you carry yourself can have a powerful effect on your attitude; and as we all know, bringing a can-do attitude with you into the college-essay process is essential. Striking a "High-Power Pose" for just two minutes can impact how you feel about yourself and your abilities, imbuing you with confidence and decreasing your cortisol ("stress hormone") levels. Take up some space with your body, one of the hallmarks of a *high-power pose*. Might I suggest a popular stance appropriately nicknamed "The Wonder Woman" in which you stand firmly with your legs at hip distance and your hands on your hips? Or "The Salutation," in which you take that same strong stance with both hands raised upward in a V-shape toward the sun? Make a proactive move to feel more powerful and relaxed in your own skin. Then carry that newfound positive energy back with you to the essay page.

Recite Daily Affirmations

As with power posing, feeding yourself with positivity and optimism can have an astounding effect on your productivity levels.

If you wake up feeling low or find yourself stuck at any point in the process, have a conversation with yourself. I swear this is a sign of health and not insanity. Pump yourself up. Say the things you know are true, even if you don't feel them in the moment: *Today I am excited about everything. I will stop underestimating myself. I know I can trust my brain and write my guts out and trust my gut and write my brains out.* The power of these words will work their way into your thoughts and fuel your work on the page.

Are you thinking, *This is actually crazy. No person in their right mind does this.* Wrong. I'm doing it right now. *(Right this second.)* I'm looking at myself in the mirror making Arnold Schwarzenegger–style poses yelling, "I'm as majestic as a lion and as sharp as a velociraptor's claw!" And I must say, I'm feeling very confident as I finish up 90 percent of this chapter. *(Go me!)*

Still, maybe you'd rather chill out?

Meditate

Start with a beginner's breathing exercise. All you need is your body and a quiet space. Set a timer for two minutes, sit down on the floor with crossed legs—or in a chair if you lack flexibility—and count each breath. This is harder than you think; other thoughts will come into your mind, thoughts about why your second paragraph isn't working quite right and what you want to eat for dinner. *(A whole pizza?*) Push those thoughts out of your mind and simply concentrate on taking long, slow breaths. When the timer rings, open your eyes and linger in a moment of calm. Now go eat those pepperonis.

DEBUNKING THE PERFECTIONISM MYTH AND SAYING GOODBYE

There is an old adage that says, "Writing is never done, it's just due." If you look hard enough there will always be a detail you want to change, a description you can improve upon, a word that is almost but not quite right. The problem with trying to achieve perfection is that it is one of humankind's only unachievable dreams. It's the siren that calls unsuspecting writers out to sea to drown in the misery of endless revision. As Voltaire once said, "Perfect is the enemy of good." After much hard work, when you suspect you've collected a thoughtfully ordered set of words that may be your final draft, go through your final round of checks, give the essay one last read, and as Elsa, Queen of Arendelle, once famously said, "Let it go."

One last note about the overall impact of college essay writing and the application process as a whole: There is no such thing as a perfect application. Even if you submit impeccable test scores, an off-the-charts transcript, and a heartfelt masterpiece of an essay, there are still many elements involved in the application process that are simply out of your control. I know it's hard but try to go with the flow and embrace your lack of control over the end result. Trust me, you will end up where you belong. And approaching the application essay-writing process with this measured outlook will allow you to manage your stress, put the process in perspective, and be ever more yourself on the page.

10 Do You Think These People Are Boring? Essay Examples and How to Use—or Not Use—Them

As I've already mentioned, I am adamant that reading a thousand examples of successful college admissions essays is a bad idea, destined to cloud your brain and induce the panic I just helped you overcome. I still stand by this advice. That said, the internet is a candy store full of college essay examples, and even I'm tempted to indulge my essay example sweet tooth from time to time. Also, taking a peek at some writing created by real students might just help solidify the advice I've been dispensing over the course of this book. Which is why in this chapter, I'm sharing excerpts from some of my favorite college essays over the years. These passages (and my commentary) appear in bite-sized chunks meant to inspire instead of overwhelm. So use them as a point of reference, stimulation, or insight. Do NOT use them as a template, formula, or point of comparison. Remember, these excerpts showcase effective strategies and tools that you can implement in your own college essays, but you also have ideas that no one else in the history of college essay writing has ever used before. Use these examples as a guide and launch point, not a limitation.

Why don't we start from the beginning—the literal beginning of some of my favorite student essays. Below are some of the most intriguing, attention-getting, thought-provoking, curiosity-inducing, overall effective opening lines and passages I have seen in my time as an essay advisor. Would these essay introductions capture your attention and convince you this applicant is anything but boring?

MAGIC OPENING LINES/PARAGRAPHS

Most people have ten toes, but my dad only has five. When I was young, he told me he lost the digits on his left foot while climbing Aconcagua in 1982 because he couldn't afford warm mountaineering boots. While that may have been part of the reason, like many things between my dad and me, it wasn't the whole truth.

I will never forget the student whose dad only had five toes. This line has been stuck in my brain for *years*. That kind of hook has what writers *(and marketers!)* call "stickiness." It lodges itself in your brain forever *(which is very useful for an applicant looking to get noticed!)*. I also love that this student baits the reader with a cliffhanger at the end of the paragraph. It wasn't the whole truth? Tell me more!

***

Every time I step onto the ice, my goal is to make people doubt their eyesight. This is slightly ironic, given that I have wanted to be an ophthalmologist since I was five. Still, when my body is in perfect formation, engaged in endless rotation in the middle of the rink, I want people to ask themselves, "Is she really doing that?"

This student uses so many effective strategies in one short paragraph. She teases an idea in the first line that makes the reader want to know more. *(Why would people doubt their eyesight?)* She gives a clue as to how two disparate parts of her life—ice skating and ophthalmology—might connect in the larger essay. And she ends the paragraph on a hypothetical quote that really sets a scene.

***

The underside of a cross-stitched pillowcase is always surprising. While the front displays a colorful and exacting design, the back is often messy: a web of overlapped strings that belies the complexity required to create the intricate and orderly picture most people see.

Here, detailed description takes center stage, along with the setup of what is likely to be a glorious overarching metaphor. There's just a hint of what is to come in this compact opening paragraph, but as a reader I am intrigued and already trust the writer to take it home. *(Also, I can confirm, the essay delivered a glorious overarching metaphor.)*

***

My parents are a quark and an antiquark, a single unit made up of two parts whose differences complement each other. My two siblings and I are as inseparable as a baryon particle. When I'm dancing, I feel rhythm as a steady state universe and hear sad music as dark matter. The decisions I make translate into energy. Physics is the lens through which I see the world. Even the language of Newton's three laws says something about my life.

Right away, the scientific language nods to this applicant's interests and expertise. When they tell me physics is the language through which they see the world, I believe them. They've already proven it to me through their clever comparisons and writing style. I want to see how far they will take the metaphor and why this subject has so captured their heart and mind.

***

"Is this the right one?" my little sister asked, clutching my grandparents' hands, as the U-Bahn approached Alexanderplatz. I compared the number on the train to the notes I had taken in advance on the inside cover of my visitor's guide as I ushered everyone onboard. We had traveled to Berlin to experience a city rich with history and culture. Even though I was only 14 at the time, my family had left the logistics of our trip to me because that was, and is, the role I have assumed in my house.

Starting with a quote and unfolding into a scene, this student gives us so much to take in from her opening lines. She's an international traveler, leading family members from multiple generations. Why are the details of this trip being left to a fourteen-year-old? Why does she love organization so much? Did the family get on the right U-Bahn after all? I can't wait to find out.

***

Dad says I'm a Mark, but Mom thinks I'm more of a Barbara. Personally, I think I'm a Kevin, though I aspire to embody qualities of each of the self-starters on the reality show Shark Tank. *Every week, while hopeful entrepreneurs pitch their ideas to a team of high-profile investors, my family piles onto the couch, competing to calculate valuations or guess which Shark will bite.*

The snappiness of this opening always makes me smile, as does the quirkiness of the overall approach. If you are familiar with *Shark Tank*, you will likely recognize what the applicant is talking about within seconds. If not, when you are let in on what the writer is setting up, the cleverness of the idea still impresses. One thing's for sure: No other student is submitting an essay quite like this one.

***

Trudging through misty wetlands, the soldiers approach their extraction point. Suddenly, a low-pitched whoosh from a thermal detonator pierces the air. "Look out!" Enemy forces spring up, surrounding the squadron in a coordinated ambush. From the east, a regal shuttle lands directly in front of the besieged rebels. It's Admiral Thrawn and his Death Troopers. My alarm goes off. Two hours have passed, but I'm not done with my episode—"episodes" are what I call my Star Wars action figure battles. I sigh as I collect the figures, returning them to their appropriate bins: rebels, imperials, and spaceships.

I am fully invested in this battle. Even more so because, by the end of this opening paragraph, I get a strong sense of how committed the student is to these creative exercises they set up. The descriptions are so vivid, I understand what it's like to be in this person's brain, submitting completely to imagination without judgment or self-consciousness. In my opinion, to embrace this kind of an exercise takes the kind of creativity, vision, and confidence I would want in an applicant. I'm sure admissions felt the same way and couldn't wait to see where the rest of the essay adventure would take them.

***

My 13-year-old sister has described my work uniform, which consists of a black polyester t-shirt with the red AMC Dine-In logo on it, as "depressingly ugly." But it doesn't matter what I'm wearing when I'm balancing six drinks on my precarious walk to the family in row eight. At the AMC Bridgewater Dine-In 7 movie theater, I occupy one of four positions, including greeter, box office operator, drink expo worker, and support assistant. Instead of a concession stand, there is a large menu, filled with overpriced eating options. A soda costs $6. Popcorn is $8.50. Luckily, both are free while I'm on the job.

The quote from dear sister is priceless. It makes me cackle every time, and really sets the stage for what is a humor-filled examination of a fairly routine job. This is an example of how elements of a student's life that may seem pedestrian to them are fascinating to others. I am dying to know this applicant's favorite snack. How many buckets of popcorn can a person eat before they never want to eat popcorn ever again? And what else does this person learn on the job?

KILLER CLOSING LINES

What is a magic opener without a killer closer? Thankfully, none of the students who wrote the following closing lines had to find out.

Ironically, it's my years spent working in the junkyard—the place where rusty cars go to die—that has laid the foundation for my desire to pursue a career in medicine. I'm grateful to my dad's business for everything it has taught me about staying organized, but I'm also ready for a future outside of it. Instead of people calling me "Boss Lady," I'm ready for them to call me "Doctor."

Yes, this applicant did work in a junkyard, which is inherently interesting. But she also managed to connect her wild work stories to her ambitions to enter the medical field. Connecting her nickname from the junkyard *(which is a great one)* to the new name she hopes to acquire is a clever way to bring everything together.

***

If given half a chance, I will always choose the split, the cleave, the partial. I love half moons and half smiles and that feeling of being more than halfway there. Which is why it doesn't matter whether I'm celebrating a birthday or a half birthday, singing a sad song or a happy one, eating half a cake or double as much as is advisable. As long as I am surrounded by the people who matter to me, my glass is half full.

This student uses the theme of halves throughout the essay, but in the conclusion they really amp up the wordplay. While I usually discourage employing clichés, ending on one after using the word "half" in so many other creative ways ends up being unexpected, a familiar place for the reader to land that feels poetic.

***

Back in the bathroom, I abandoned the box of hair dye. I realized that I am comfortable being myself. There's no such thing as "supposed to be." There is only "what is," and the determination to make the most of life's unexpected turns. Now I know, if I'm willing to look for it, every silver hair will have a silver lining.

This is another example where an unexpected use of a cliché in wordplay really lands the plane. *(Look at me breaking my own rules all over the place.)* The student's essay discussed how they grappled with the very early graying of their hair, which started at age fourteen. A heartfelt, straightforward reflection on the moment they decided to embrace their true hair color combined with some clever wordsmithing puts a *(silver?)* bow on a gold-star essay.

***

Dear Journal,
Today, a year and a half after visiting China, I received another gift. It contained four boxes of chocolates, the kind Li introduced me to when I first arrived in China. As I bit into a piece, I was transported back to Xi'an. I keep thinking about how, in China, food allowed me to gain my footing and expand my borders. Sharing meals with my host family made me feel less like an outsider and immersed me in community ritual. Learning to leave the second egg for my host sister brought

me closer to a culture through expanded understanding and empathy. Food is an entry point. It will always help me understand the world around me and make the foreign feel more familiar.

Not everyone can pull off an essay that deviates from a more standard form, but this student did just that. The conclusion maintains what we can assume has been an ongoing journal format, presenting internal monologue in the present tense and calling back to sweet *(see what I did there)* references from earlier anecdotes that illustrate the applicant's immersion in and appreciation of their surroundings. The creativity and adeptness with which this was executed impressed admissions officers enough to send the applicant their own delicious gift of acceptance. *(They may have even written about the cleverness of the student's approach in their own journals!)*

***

I think about these things as Ruth raises a shaky arm and cries out "Bingo" with all the enthusiasm of a high-stakes game. I help her up from her seat and lead her to the front, where Wendy hands her a prize—a bottle of lavender hand cream. As she sits back down, cradling her precious win, I wonder about all the small things I have yet to encounter. When I am Ruth's age, what will I look back on and remember with fondness? Life is textured by these details, and I'm excited to discover my own.

I fell in love with all of these senior citizens playing bingo as I read this student's essay. I also felt quite endeared to the student, who showed their investment in this community and ability to see the magic in everyday interactions. I hope Ruth enjoyed her lavender hand cream.

ESSAYS I LOVED

To give you a more comprehensive peek at some of the more successful college admissions essays I've seen, I have chosen a few of my favorites, summarized their messages, and included some of the best sections from each. These essays inspired admissions officers to accept the students in question. My guess is you'll want to meet these students, too. *(As you might guess, they—and their essays—are pretty darn interesting.)*

(Please note, these titles are the shorthand I created for each essay [à la "Plant Mom"], not titles given to the essays by the students themselves. Most students

I work with don't use a title, opting to let the prompt lead right into the story. Though you can add a title to your work if you so choose.)

Dad Has Five Toes

Most people have ten toes, but my dad only has five. When I was young, he told me he lost the digits on his left foot while climbing Aconcagua in 1982 because he couldn't afford warm mountaineering boots. While that may have been part of the reason, like many things between my dad and me, it wasn't the whole truth.

I had to isolate this opening paragraph with the magic openers *(because it's that good)* and include a deeper dive into the essay here. This student uses his personal statement to talk about his father—a victim of childhood trauma—and how his dad's response to that trauma made him both a good and bad example to follow. Notably, he avoids the common pitfall of making the entire essay about his dad's life by focusing on their relationship and what he learned from it.

I particularly love this description of what the author calls "Type 1 Fun" and "Type 2 Fun," a very personal and intriguing perspective.

One of the most valuable things my father did was introduce me to the idea of "Type 2 Fun." Unlike "Type 1 Fun," which is easily enjoyed in the moment, "Type 2 Fun" centers around challenge and delayed gratification. In fact, "Type 2 Fun" can be downright unpleasant while you're experiencing it. You're at 10,000 feet, knee-deep in snow. No matter how many layers you have piled on, you're shivering so hard that you daydream about being by a fireplace. You can't feel your feet as you huddle behind a rock to try and take a bite out of a peanut butter and jelly sandwich that is frozen solid. All for the possibility of standing atop a mountain. To me, though the ascent to the summit lasts a few minutes and the torturous climb lasts for days, the feeling of accomplishment is completely worth it.

The applicant goes on to address what he has learned from his own pursuit of "Type 2 Fun."

Climbing is all about risk management. You have to know your limits because success is defined as much by your retreats as it is by your ascents.

Finally, he defines himself on his own terms.

Unlike my father, through mountaineering I've learned to overcome obstacles and embrace failure. I challenge myself not because I have anything to prove, but because I want to know my own limits and test them. I now realize that when my father tried to avoid becoming like his own dad, he only succeeded in making different mistakes that created a similar chasm between him and the rest of his family. In some ways, I am a reflection of my father: in my interests and certain qualities of which I am proud. But it's not all or nothing. I can take the good and leave the bad. Because life is not black and white, or failure and success. The real value lies in the gray areas.

This student has successfully reached the peak of college essay writing, that is for sure.

The Nike Jordans

Using dialogue as a main component in setting up her opening scene, this student introduces the idea that maybe, just maybe, people in America have some misconceptions about her home country of Senegal.

> *The first time I was really puzzled by a question about my African origins I was shopping in a mall in Maryland. One of the sales clerks complimented me on my sneakers, asking me where I got them. I told her that I bought them overseas in my country: Senegal. "They have Nike Jordans in Africa?" she asked me. She was surprised that I would be able to purchase the same products in Africa that are available in America.*

The writer goes on to recount various examples of the same kind of misunderstanding and miscommunication, relaying her own shock and awe as various Americans she meets during a gap year in Washington, DC, confirm her suspicions that her culture and upbringing are grossly misunderstood by the average American, defined by an array of disturbing clichés.

> *Her reaction was not the last strange comment or inaccurate assumption I encountered during my adventures abroad. In a restaurant in Washington, DC, I was waiting for my order when I revealed to the waitress that I was from Africa. She exclaimed, "Really? That's so cool. When I was younger* The Lion King *was my favorite movie." One man in Florida asked me how I managed to travel to the States, taking on an embarrassed shade of beet red after I said, "a plane!" And an old lady shared her regret of never experiencing a safari, and was dumbfounded that I myself had never seen a giraffe or any other exotic animals. (I live in a bustling metropolis.) The comments and questions that came up most often were regarding my language and manner of speaking. Some people seemed surprised*

that I did not have an accent, considering it was my first time in the US. Others were just puzzled that I spoke French instead of "African."

Still, the student's response to these bizarre encounters is not one of anger or frustration, but one of hope and understanding. In fact, it motivates her to become a proactive force for change in bridging the gap between these cultures.

While some people would have been offended by such questions and comments, I believe this dialogue is proof of a communication and knowledge gap rather than general insensitivity. Each bizarre inquiry and assumption taught me more about the deeply ingrained beliefs and false perceptions people have about my country— beliefs I can help adjust.

She closes with a line that showcases perspective, maturity, and grace, qualities that attract any admissions counselor, and leaves the reader with food for thought.

The more proactively curious we are about other people's backgrounds, the more informed and open-minded we become. Along the way, the most valuable thing we can do is show understanding for each other as we stumble along the road to world knowledge and cultural sensitivity—after all, who among us already knows it all?

An expertly executed ending, to say the least.

Maple Taffy

There are very few people who don't have personal connections to and associations with food, so this student's strategy to connect various landmark phases of her life with related food items was sure to resonate with readers.

I was born in the birthplace of maple taffy, raised on the island of tea sandwiches, and matured into adulthood in the land of Betty Crocker. My identity is multilayered and directly connected to the contents of my stomach. Who I am is what I have eaten.

The writer goes on to describe the previously teased food items and what they signify in her life.

My parents and entire extended family originate from Canada, which is why one of my first memories as a child involves tire d'erable *(maple taffy). This classic*

Canadian treat is essentially heated maple syrup, poured over packed snow. Once tacky, the solidifying syrup is gathered up on a popsicle stick to be eaten much like a lollipop. As many impatient two-year-olds and their parents will tell you, if you roll up the taffy before it's ready, you will have a sticky situation on your hands. (Literally!) In fact, there is a picture of me sitting on our living room mantle, with my toddler hands covered in this sugary goo. When I look at that image, I can almost smell the maple syrup and hear my relatives gathering around the holiday table in the country where I entered the world.

It was a cupcake that marked my official entry into life as an American. The cupcake itself was as all-American as they come, baked from a Betty Crocker cake mix and topped with white frosting, red sprinkles, and a toothpick bearing a miniature American flag. My school principal made them for my sister and me in celebration of our newly bestowed citizenship.

To wrap things up, the writer provides insight into what it's like to hail from three disparate places and cultures.

Having close ties to three different countries, I have often struggled with self-identification. I was born in Canada but lived there for the least amount of time. I spent my formative childhood years in Ireland, but still only resided there for three years. Then, I moved to America, but did not obtain citizenship until ten years later. Even before I became a bona fide American, on trips back to Montreal, people would often question if I was a "true Canadian." I have come to realize that my identity can be as complex as my palate.

What admissions officer wouldn't want to admit someone who can find sweetness wherever their next adventure takes them?

What Makes a Woman

One of the most intimate and thoughtful essays I've ever read comes from a student who wrote about her experience of being acutely aware of her body's development right around the time her mother was diagnosed with breast cancer. She opens with this line:

Through my 13-year-old eyes, maturity was proportionate to cup size.

The writer then moves on to illustrate the concurrent developments in her teenage life and the life of her mother. This is an incredible example of how a student can write about a person who inspired them and who has had a great effect on their lives while still revealing an ocean's worth of information about themselves. Take this excerpt toward the end of this essay:

> *As her treatments continued, we found out that my mom would need to undergo a double mastectomy. She recognized that the physical transformation of her body was going to be drastic and that it would take some getting used to, but she also reassured me that nothing fundamental about her would change. This contradicted what I had come to believe—that the development of one's body was the primary indicator of true womanhood. In the weeks that followed my mom's surgery, I came to understand that a woman is not defined by her physical traits. Seeing Mom wear shirts that showed off her flat chest, I could tell that she was proud of herself for surviving cancer, and more importantly, had embraced her life-changing experience. I was incredibly proud of her, too.*

The student continues her exploration of what it means to gain a symbol of womanhood while her mother gives one up, and how this affects her worldview.

> *At 17, I have a new understanding of what it means to be a woman. While womanhood and adulthood can be hard to define, they are states characterized by far more than one's anatomy. Being a woman means making independent decisions and being confident in oneself. Being a woman is about understanding one's strengths and weaknesses, and recognizing the uphill battle one may face in a less-than-perfect world. Being a woman means not letting someone else define womanhood for you.*

I know. Catch your breath. Wipe your tears. She's amazing. Who wouldn't want to have this young woman on their campus?

The Air Traveler

This student had me at his relatable first sentence and immediate script-flipping.

> *Most people dread going to the airport, but to me there is nothing more thrilling.*

How can anyone love the airport? He immediately elaborates, providing a deeply immersive sense of place:

> *I love Istanbul Airport, where my senses are activated by buzzing crowds and aromas of delicious food. Hunting for Lufthansa aircraft models and Kinder Eggs*

at the Frankfurt Airport gift shops always excites me. And nothing feels more like home than riding the chimney-shaped people movers at Virginia's Dulles International Airport.

We learn over the course of the essay that each of the airports described is significant, connecting to a personal passion and element of this student's heritage:

> I believe air travel should be welcoming and accessible to all regardless of background, age, or ability. This impulse to envision a transportation system centered around the good of the collective is rooted in my Turkish heritage; I lived in Turkey from the second through ninth grades and when I return, I am always reminded of how highly Turks value friendship and interaction.

It becomes clear that this is a student with a passion for aviation and engineering, which is demonstrated by his technical language and the examples he chooses to back up his statements.

> Efficiency is also essential to air travel, from in-airport transportation to an airplane's engineering. My drive for efficiency is most connected to my German side, where my mother has her roots. At Frankfurt Airport, boarding is organized to perfection and rules enable orderly flow through checkpoints...This meticulousness and precision are reflected in my work, whether I am generating flight route simulations with geospatial data for my engineering research or carefully crafting videos about how to engineer a sustainable aircraft.

But this is an essay not all engineering students could write. It is differentiated by the focus on his background and unique perspective, even as he uses the space to elaborate on his extensive experience in the field and self-motivated, aviation-related education.

> Air travel's inherent emphasis on inclusion is where my American side comes in. Here, I feel accepted and embraced for my unique background in a way I have not anywhere else. Perhaps it is because of my need to adapt every time I move back and forth between countries that I appreciate how American culture embraces diversity. I have strived to foster the inclusion of students from all backgrounds in my outreach work for the nonprofit Youth Aviation Adventure, creating educational videos that explain concepts such as "how planes fly." As someone who grew up spending nearly every weekend at the Air and Space Museum, I want to share that feeling of curiosity and possibility with young people all over the world.

Finally, this applicant ends with a clever reflection on what his experience means for his future.

> *Just like the sensation of flying—that moment right before a plane lifts its wheels from the runway—never gets old, neither will the knowledge that my background will speed me toward a future of invention, one that I hope makes air travel a thrill for all to experience.*

And just like that, an admissions officer's fear of flying—and any doubts they may have had about admitting this student—have disappeared.

In the Car with Mom

Another one of my favorite essays comes from an applicant who reflects on what an average daily activity like a routine car ride means for her family connections and personal growth. The student opens her essay with vivid lines of dialogue, effectively setting the scene and revealing a lot about the characters in the process.

> "What did you dream about last night?" Mom asks me.
>
> It is 5:25 a.m., and my mother is still in her pajamas, huddled in a big sweatshirt to combat the winter cold. She is barely awake, and though I am only slightly more alive, as we sit next to each other in the car, we feel a desire to engage.
>
> "I was sliding down a laundry chute," I tell her, "dodging these crazy obstacles to get to the end and see what was waiting for me."
>
> We sit together in silence for a moment.
>
> "What did you dream about?" I ask in return.
>
> "I was driving around with Prince Harry and Prince William, taking them for a sightseeing tour of New York; I have no idea why. I was probably thinking I had to get up to drive you."
>
> "See, you are a born chauffeur," I tease.

The applicant goes on to explore what this time in the car with her mother each morning meant to her, what it taught her, and what she realized when it inevitably came to a close. She writes,

> *In 2013 I passed my road test, and my whole routine changed. Communal conversation became personal reflection. Now, after practice I run through vocabulary words in my head alone, without a motherly prompt. I contemplate*

my future without side opinions. Most recently, I find myself thinking through my college options, all without my trusty sounding board in the driver's seat. Though her commentary comes less frequently and later in the day, I still know she will always tell me exactly what she thinks. There are moments when I feel lost without her in the morning. Then I realize participating in those morning car rides was the ultimate form of preparation. Now I belong in the driver's seat.

This essay reveals how a simple concept can be extremely meaningful when addressed with overwhelming self-assuredness and heart.

Stacey's Final Thoughts

My dearest applicants, we have made it through the college essay-writing and advising process together, and I now consider you to be friends and fellow essay experts. Know this: I believe you have an "uncommon" story within you that is as personal and authentic to you as any of the stories detailed in this book. I actually *know* you do. So if you find yourself second-guessing your writing abilities or the value of your lived experiences thus far, knock it off and come back here for a dose of inspiration and encouragement. Because you, my friend, are not boring. And I can't wait to hear all the stories you'll tell.

Want to show me your essay draft or need some additional help getting started? Visit collegeessayadvisors.com for more free resources and to get advice from a member of my expert team!

Acknowledgments

I wrote this book in a manner I would discourage most applicants from following for literally anything: at a breakneck pace and on an impossible deadline. I wouldn't have been able to succeed without the following whip-smart, unconditionally supportive crew.

Thank you first and foremost to my students, who allowed me to hone my craft and do what I love most. Thank you Jasmine Faustino, without whose publishing/editing savvy, guidance, and friendship I would have been lost. Melanie Ashkar, you are my word fairy godmother, always coming through in the clutch. Thank you for your eagle eye, collaborative spirit, and unfailing commitment to this book. Rachael Fendrich, thank you for being such a bright light, brilliant problem solver, and editorial anchor. Thanks to Nathan Davidson for your vision, and to Jasmine Holman, Christopher Fischer, Anne Hunt, Rae-Ann Goodwin, and the teams at Bloomsbury and Integra for your hard work in bringing this project to fruition.

A collection of people I love and whom I can never thank enough for being in my life: Cindy Wen, Dave Pucino, Katy Chrisler, Jasmine Bible, Rae Heller, Peggy Intrator, Julia Pimsleur, Melissa Bank, James Heaney, Michael Ventura, Vannessa Seacrest, Lisa Landsberg, Erica Kung, Punita Bhansali, Sarah Gowrie, Joy Ritumala, Hannah Detsis, Megan Fleming, Pia Silva Wasterval, Josh Hawkins, Carolyn Balbo, and Zoe Nehrer.

To Judi Mogen, my work/life mom: How lucky are we to have found each other? I would not be here without you, nor would I want to be. A carrot cake to celebrate? To Becca Myers, my work/life sister: Thank you for being my lifeline and one of the only people who understands me down to the fibers of my being. We are going to make so many t-shirts this year. To Kat Stubing, my work/life forever partner: No, I will never let you go. You are too good at everything. I could not possibly love spending my working days with anyone more, and cannot wait for our future adventures and hours-long conversations about nothing/everything.

Thanks to my family, my forever heart. Rachel and Rob, congratulations, lovebirds (!) and please ignore any potential legal issues you find as you read. Adam and Alli, I love you weirdos and, yes, I will help Frankie write his college barkmissions essay. Mom, thanks for knowing I was a college essay expert before I did, and for buying me the dress in my author photo (obviously). I learned how to be a Boss (with a capital "B") from you. Dad, maybe one of the Mets' kids needs essay help? Want to nudge them my way from wherever you are? I miss you deeply. Carol and George, look what those Covid-era phone calls hath wrought. (Thanks for putting up with them, and me!) Ellen, Maddy, and Emmie, I love you all so much (and yes, the college essay help is here for you when you need it). Grandma…look what I did!

Jeffrey-chan. How did I get so lucky? Thank you for being so darn brilliant/curious/adorable, and for perfectly modeling how to work and live in balance. I love life with you.

Thank you to the city of Tokyo for serving as my writing lab and constant inspiration. Your noodles got me through the toughest edits.

I also want to dedicate this book to my favorite writing teachers over the years. Thanks to Arlene Dorfman (Dorfie!) for assigning an essay about *Our Town* that inspired my first teenage stab at satire, and for tapping into my performer instincts; to Dottie Clark (Professor Clark!) for encouraging me to embrace my emerging voice and pop culture sensibilities; and to Marilyn Root (DocR!) for helping me hone my confidence, persuasive powers, and conversational tone. I think about all three of you regularly as I teach and write, and if I inspire anyone even close to as much as you all inspired me, I will have achieved a lifelong goal.

Index

abbreviations, use of 77
accomplishment essay 19–20
accuracy, editing for 75–6
Activity Essay 88–9
Additional Information, prompt 100
Additional Information Essay 98–100
admissions
    and overall application 5–6
    reading college essay 6–7
admissions essays. *See* supplemental essays
admissions officer 1–2, 4–6, 11, 34, 52, 55, 61, 69–70, 73, 79, 113, 130, 136
    and authenticity 111
    avoiding cliches for 77
    and background prompt 14
    and beliefs prompt 17–18
    and branding 111
    editing for clarity for 74
    employing wordplay for 74
    and Gargantuan Four 36
    grabbing attention of 6–7
    last line of essay for 66–7
    lists read by 107
    making oneself memorable to 7, 25
    making smile 112
    and other admissions essays 83–104
    and passion prompt 20
    plagiarism and AI 109
    preparing opening line for 61–4
    and prompts 13
    putting personality on display for 8
    showing sincerity to 33
    showing *versus* telling in relation to 107
    telling admissions something they don't know 7–8
    valuing quirks 106
    writing middle of essay for 64–6
admissions takeaway, Gargantuan Four 35–6
AI. *See* artificial intelligence
"Air Travel, The," excerpt 135–6
artificial intelligence (AI) 109–10
authentic *versus* quirky 32–3, 106

background, writing about 14–15
background prompt
    background 14–15
    identity 15
    interests 16
    overview 14
    questions for 14
    talents 16
Backwards Brainstorm 37
    dos and don'ts 31–3
    finding winning topic 36
    Gargantuan Four 33–6
    getting active 30
    getting started 24–5
    hunting for milestones 30
    listing things you love/hate 25–30
    narrowing down topics 33–4
    working through being boring 23–4
beginning, tying ending back to 65
beige, listing 25–30
being cozy, listing 25–30
being too cold/hot, listing 25–30
beliefs prompts 17–18
Big Three, groupings 33–4
books, listing 25–30
brainstorming time, failing to put in 32

break, taking 118
Brook, Stacey 1–2, 41

CEA. *See* College Essay Advisors
Challenges and Circumstances, prompt 98–100
clarity, editing for 74–5
cliches, using 77
cliffhanger, avoiding 67
closing line, writing 66–8
college application, essay in 5–6
college essay
    decoding personal essay 11–22
    dispelling misconceptions of 105–13
    excerpts 125–38
    finding magic topic 23–37
    finishing touches 71–81
    Freewriting Your Face Off 39–53
    importance of 3–9
    introduction to 1–2
    misconceptions of 39
    other admissions essays 83–104
    Sculpting Your Story 55–70
    staying sane while writing 115–24
College Essay Advisors (CEA) 1, 113
common causes of writer's block
    constant distraction 117
    fear of failure 116
    not having enough/having too much to do 116–17
common errors, looking for 76–7
communities, writing about 90–1
Community Essay 89–91
community member, proving value as 8
confirmation, looking for 65
constant distraction 117
creativity, handling 33
Cuddy, Amy 123

"Dad Has Five Toes," excerpt 131–2
daily affirmations, reciting 123
details, digging for 31
dialogue, diving into 72
dialogue, opening with 62
Didion, Joan 41
differentiating factor, Gargantuan Four 34–5
digital detox 119

dinner, listing 25–30
disconnection 40
Diversity Essay 92–4
Doctorow, E. L. 41
don'ts (of college essays)
    adding extra words 108
    negativity 108
    quirky *versus* authentic 106
    repeating resume 107
    ruling out ideas 106
    selling oneself short 108
    showing *versus* telling 107
    skipping final edit 109
    writing about intangible qualities 106–7
dos and don'ts
    Backwards Brainstorm 31–3
    closing line 66–8
    opening line 62–4
dos (of college essays)
    authenticity 111
    branding 111
    calculated risks 111
    calling for help 113
    choosing advisers wisely 111–12
    entertaining admissions officer 112
    listening to gut 112
    organizing work 110
    relatively random nature of process 112–13
    starting early 110
Drill Around/Down 42–3
Duke University 87

Emory University 95
emotions, letting out 122
excerpts (of college essays)
    examples 130–7
    killer closing lines 128–30
    magic opening lines/paragraphs 125–8
extra words, adding 108

failure, fear of 116
failure prompt 16–17
fears, compartmentalizing 40–1
Febos, Melissa 41
filling, Sculpting Your Story 57–8
final edit, skipping 109
first-person storytelling. *See* personal essay

flipping, Sculpting Your Story 57
Freewriting Your Face Off
    defining freewriting 41–2
    drilling around/down 42–3
    essay mapping 52–3
    example prompts 45–8
    finding patterns 48–50
    identifying highlights 51–2
    outlining 52–3
    overview 39
    plucking gems 50–1
    rules 43–5
    setting mood 40–1
    soliciting prompts 44–8

Gargantuan Four 33–6, 61, 70
gems, plucking 50–1
Georgetown University 101–2
getting active 30
glasses, listing 25–30
GPA. *See* grade point average
grade point average (GPA) 5
grammar, forgetting 44

hanger 121
happy place, finding 40
Harvard University 89
having too much to do 116–17
highlights, identifying 51–2
High-Power Pose, striking 123
hopelessly stressed/blocked, cures for 122–4
humor, adding 73
humor, kicking of essay with 62
hunger, combatting 121
hydration 121

I, word 12
ideas. *See also* college essay; prompts
    narrowing down 36
    prompt solicitation 44–5
    quirky *versus* authentic 32, 106
    ruling out 106
    trashing 32
identity, writing about 15
independent platforms, submitting essays through 101–4
inner critic, silencing 117

inspiration, seeking 41
instincts, forgetting 32
intangible qualities, writing about 106–7
interests, writing about 16
"In the Car with Mom," excerpt 137
intrigue, editing for
    asking questions 72
    diving into dialogue 72
    humor 73
    sincerity 73
    wordplay 74

Jamison, Leslie 41
judgment, removing 31–2

killer closing lines 128–30

language, keeping active 64
last line, importance of 66–8
laundry, listing 25–30
lay of the land (of college essay)
    admissions officers 6–7
    essay in overall application 5–6
    importance of college essay 4–5
    making oneself memorable 7–9
    overview 3–4
lists 25–30
loose draft, composing 58–60

magic opening lines/paragraphs 125–8
main point, building 64–6
"Maple Taffy," excerpt 133–4
mapping (your essay) 52–3
Massachusetts Institute of Technology 102–4
maximum efficiency, organizing supplements for 100–1
mechanism, personal essay 69
meditation 123–4
metaphor, personal essay 68–9
milestones, hunting for 30
misconceptions, debunking
    college essay don'ts 106–9
    college essay dos 110–3
    overview 105
    plagiarism 109–10
modern art and architecture, listing 25–30

mood, setting
　compartmentalizing fears 40–1
　disconnection 40
　finding happy place 40
　seeking inspiration 41
moving 122
music, listing 25–30

narcissism, embracing 31
negativity, averting 108
"Nike Jordans, The," excerpt 132–3
Northwestern University 91
not having enough 116–17

Oddball Essay 94–6
opening line, dos and don'ts of writing 61–4
optionality 98
outlining (your essay) 52–3
overarching message, Gargantuan Four 35
over-vocabularization 76–7

parental input/takeover 33
passion prompt 20–1
patterns, finding 48–50
perfectionism myth, debunking 124
personal essay
　accomplishment essay 19–20
　background prompt 14–16
　beliefs prompt 17–18
　new lens for 68–9
　overview of 11–12
　passion prompt 20–1
　prompts for 13–22
　setback/failure prompt 16–17
　structure of 60–1
　topic of choice 21–2
personality, representing 7–8
personal lens, personal essay 69
personal statement. *See* personal essay
pizza, listing 25–30
plagiarism 109–10
plans, cancelling 120
"Plant Mom," essay 62, 65–6, 68–9, 72, 81
plants, listing 25–30
Polishing to Perfection
　accuracy 75–6
　clarity 74–5

editing for intrigue 72–4
final draft 79–81
most common errors 76–7
overview 71
submit button 77–9
Triple Edit 71–2
Pomona College 95
positives, focusing 120–1
power pose, striking 123
procrastination 120–1
procrastination doom loop 118
prompts (for personal essay)
　accomplishment essay 19–20
　in Additional Information Essay 98–100
　background prompt 14–16
　beliefs prompt 17–18
　overview of 13
　passion prompt 20–1
　setback/failure prompt 16–17
　soliciting 44–8
　topic of choice 21–2
proofreading. *See* accuracy, editing for

questions, asking 62, 72
quirky *versus* authentic 32–3, 106
quotes, using 63

readers. *See* admissions officer
　leaving wanting more 67
　surprising 63
Real Housewives of Anywhere, listing 25–30
reflection, ending on 67
resume, repeating 107
Rice University 87
rules, breaking 63

sanity, maintaining 121–2
Saunders, George 41
saying something that hasn't been said 7–8
scenery, change 118
Scripps College 94
Sculpting Your Story
　building main point 64–6
　collecting freewrites 55–8
　composing loose draft 58–60
　dos and don'ts 62–4

final tests 70
last line importance 66–8
new lens 68–9
opening line 61–4
overview 55
structure of personal essay 60–61
Sedaris, David 41
self-criticism, removing 31–2
setback prompt 16–17
setup, writing 65
short answers 96–8
showing *versus* telling 107
sincerity, handling 33, 73
650 words, ways to accomplish count of
    proving value as community member 8
    putting personality on display 8
    representing personality 7
    saying something that hasn't been said 7–8
    showcasing basic writing/storytelling abilities 8–9
slow walkers, listing 25–30
small details, harnessing power of 65–6
small victories, setting up opportunities 118
sneezing, listing 25–30
snipping, Sculpting Your Story 57
spelling, forgetting 44
standards, lowering 117
starting early 120
starting over 118–9
story, sculpting. *See* Sculpting Your Story
storytelling abilities, showcasing 8–9
street fairs, listing 25–30
stressful process, staying sane during
    cures for hopelessly stressed/blocked 122–4
    debunking perfectionism myth 124
    maintaining sanity 121–2
    overview 115–16
    procrastination 120
    writer's block 116–20
submit button, reviewing essay before submitting 77–9
    getting fresh pair of eyes 78
    picking prompt 78

    taking break 77
    test questions 78–9
supplemental essays
    Activity Essay 88–9
    Additional Information Essay 98–100
    Community Essay 89–91
    definition 84
    Diversity Essay 92–4
    Oddball Essay 94–6
    organizing for maximum efficiency 100–1
    overview 83–4
    short answers 96–8
    submitting essays through independent platforms 101–4
    Why Essay 84–8
Swarthmore College 93–4

talents, writing about 16
"test-optional" policy 3
"Thank You for Your Consideration," ending essay for 67
third-person perspective 12
topic, choosing
    dos and don'ts 31–3
    finding winning topic 36
    Gargantuan Four 33–6
    getting active 30
    getting started 24–5
    hunting for milestones 30
    listing things you love/hate 25–30
    narrowing down topics 33–4
    working through being boring 23–4
topic of choice 21–2
topics
    drilling around/down 42–3
    finding winning topics 36
    Gargantuan Four 34
    narrowing down 33–4
transitions, crafting 65
Triple Edit 71–2
    accuracy 75–6
    clarity 74–5
    intrigue 72–4
Tufts University 91
Twain, Mark 41

UMass Amherst 87
Uncommon College Essay Approach 1–2
    decoding personal essay 11–22
    finding magic topic 23–37
    Freewriting Your Face Off 39–53
    getting lay of the land 3–9
    Polishing to Perfection 71–81
    Sculpting Your Story 55–70
University of California 102–4
University of Chicago 94–6
University of Florida 88–9
University of Maryland 97
University of Michigan 86–7
University of Virginia 92–3
University of Wisconsin-Madison 87

vacation, listing 25–30

waiting in line, listing 25–30
Washington University 91

"What Makes a Woman," excerpt 134–5
Why Essay 84
    focusing on experiences for 86–7
    pro tip for 88
    research for 85–6
    shapeshifting question of 85
    visiting schools for 85–6
winning topic, finding 36
word count, increasing 108
wordplay, employing 74
world travel, listing 25–30
writer's block
    common causes of 116–17
    preventing 119–20
    tips for kicking 117–19
writing 43–4
writing abilities, showcasing 8–9
writing every day 119

About the Author

Stacey Brook is a writer and the founder and chief advisor at College Essay Advisors (CEA). Her work has been published in the *New Yorker*, *Teen Vogue*, *Oprah*, *McSweeney's*, *Condé Nast Traveler*, and more. Stacey and her team at CEA have been helping students tell their "uncommon" stories to admissions for over two decades. She resides in New York City, though she can often be spotted in Japan (face-deep in a bowl of noodles).